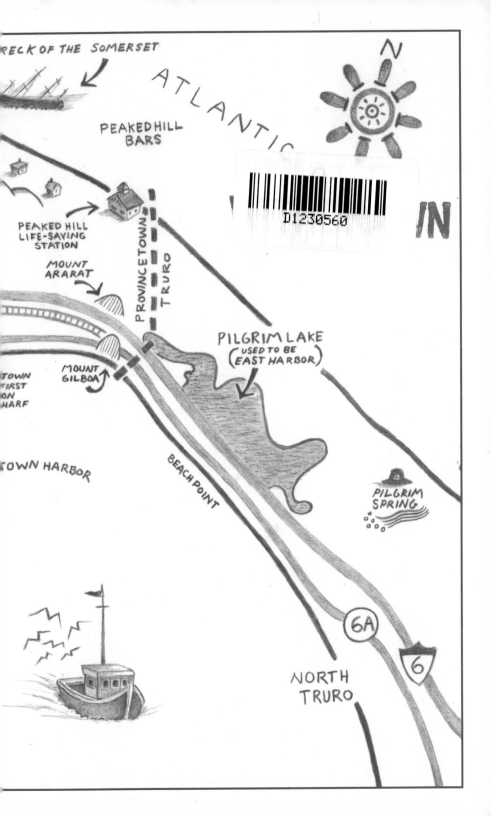

RECK OF THE SOMERSET

ATLANTIC

N

PEAKED HILL
BARS

PEAKED HILL
LIFE-SAVING
STATION

PROVINCETOWN

TRURO

MOUNT
ARARAT

PILGRIM LAKE
(USED TO BE
EAST HARBOR)

TOWN
FIRST
ION
HARF

MOUNT
GILBOA

TOWN HARBOR

BEACH POINT

PILGRIM
SPRING

6A

6

NORTH
TRURO

Provincetown

STORIES FROM LAND'S END

---

town memoirs (toun mem'wärs). 1. True stories that capture the spirit of a community, its genius loci. 2. Anecdotes passed on within a community from generation to generation. 3. A series of books by regional storytellers, illustrated by local artists, preserving the popular history of great American towns.

Provincetown

STORIES FROM LAND'S END

A MASSACHUSETTS TOWN MEMOIR

BY KATHY SHORR • Illustrated by Anne Rosen

COMMONWEALTH EDITIONS

Beverly, Massachusetts

❖ DEDICATION ❖

For Buddy Two Shoes,
King of the Dance Floor and the Editing Pencil

ISBN 1-889833-33-9

Town Memoirs series editor: Liz Nelson
Cover and text designer: Jill Feron/Feron Design
Printed in Canada.

Commonwealth Editions is an imprint of Memoirs Unlimited, Inc.,
21 Lothrop Street, Beverly, Massachusetts 01915.
Visit our Web site at www.commonwealtheditions.com.

❖ CONTENTS ❖

Acknowledgments vii
Provincetown History at a Glance viii

1620
They Came Here First 3

EIGHTEENTH CENTURY
Helltown 9
Mooncussers 11
Sand Taking Over Provincetown 12
He Should Have Stayed Home 15
No Dogs in Church, No Methodists in Town 17
The Wreck of the *Somerset* 18

NINETEENTH CENTURY
Not Walking the Plank 23
Chip Hill 25
Telling the Locals Apart 27
Mount Ararat and Mount Gilboa .28
Floating Houses 29
Lost Laundry 31
The Voyage of the *Alcyone* 33
Lancy Mansion 35
A Dem Big Splesh 37
Fourteen Numbered but Unnamed Graves 39
Town Crier 40
Professor Ready and the Sea Serpent 43
Message in a Bottle 44
Names and Directions 46
Ghosts of the Portland Gale 47
Out with the Old, in with the New 49

TWENTIETH CENTURY
The Birth of an Art Colony 53
Viola Cook 56
The Building of the Pilgrim Monument 59

The *Rose Dorothea* 63
The Boston Post Cane 66
The Back Side 68
Surfman First Class Nancy, the Life-Saving Horse 68
The Provincetown Players 71
Eugene O'Neill, German Spy? 73
The Best Dressed House in Town 75
Judge Welsh's Wrong Number 77
The *Margie III* 78
The Trial of Little Timmy 81
A Late Christmas Present 82
An Ambulance Ride 83
Snow Days 85
The Wreck of the *S-4* 86
Skully-Jo 89
The Big Beach Cleanup 89
The Cross on Long Point 92
The Blessing of the Fleet 93
The Useful Barkeep 95
The "Boys Problem" 96
Jan Muller's Wedding 97
The Birth of the Cape Cod National Seashore 98
The Night the *Advocate* Editor Got Busted 101
Desperate Living 103
Woman in the Dunes 104
A Whale of an Industry 105
A Night at The Movies 107
Life-Saving Station on the Move 109
The Meat Rack 111
The Flying Neutrinos 112
A Public Secret 114
Spiritus 115
Hurricane Bob 116
Carnival 119
The Dune Shacks 120

Sources 125

❖ ACKNOWLEDGMENTS ❖

Provincetown is one of the most *storied* places I've ever run across. I am sure this is partly because it has played an important role in American history—as the first landing place of the Pilgrims, as a center of New England's fishing and whaling, as the birthplace of the modern American theater, to name only a few. But I also think it's because things just seem to happen in Provincetown more than they do in other places. So it was not hard to dig up stories about the town, so much as it was to find ones that, for me, could capture its spirit. I suspect that most people who've spent time here have their own equally compelling tales of Provincetown, or know an aspect of a story that's missing from the version you will find here. That is, in a curious way, a satisfying thought, for it says something about the extraordinary nature of this place.

Attempting even an informal history without being a historian demands a lot of help. Thanks to Webster Bull and Liz Nelson of Commonwealth Editions, who offered an organizing framework, steady encouragement, and a gently fluctuating deadline, and proved that writers can have a pleasurable relationship with their publishers. Many people provided source material and general food for thought, in particular Debbie DeJonker of the Provincetown Library, Jeffory Morris at the Pilgrim Monument & Provincetown Museum, Napi Van Dereck, Lillian Orlowsky, Ruth Hiebert, and Julie Schecter. Chuck Turley and Laurel Guadazno at the Pilgrim Monument & Provincetown Museum and Dan Towler were kind enough to wade through early versions of the manuscript, and to share their vastly superior knowledge of Provincetown history. Arne Manos introduced me to both illustrator Anne Rosen and the last great dirt roads in town. Thanks to the *Provincetown Banner,* where an earlier version of "A Public Secret" appeared, and to the invisible readers who live in my mind while I'm working: in this case, Reuben and Judy Stern, Necee Regis, Linda Legters, and Robert Finch. Finally, I must thank my father, who, though he tried to talk me out of moving to Provincetown in 1982, did, in the end, cosign the bank loan to make it possible. Sometimes actions do speak louder than words.

—Kathy Shorr, March 2002

1004 The Viking Thorwald may have landed at what is now Provincetown.

1602 Explorer Bartholomew Gosnold named the Cape's tip "Cape Cod" after the abundant cod he found there.

1620 The *Mayflower* landed in Provincetown Harbor. The Pilgrims drafted and signed the Mayflower Compact and spent five weeks exploring the Outer Cape, before moving to Plymouth.

1727 Provincetown was named and incorporated after an uncomfortable thirteen years as a precinct of Truro.

1837 The salt-making industry in Provincetown reached its height, producing almost 50,000 bushels of sea salt a year.

1840s Portuguese sailors and fishermen began to arrive in Provincetown to work on fishing and whaling vessels, quickly displacing Yankees in these industries.

1860s In Provincetown's "Golden Era," the town dominated the Cape's fishing industry. In 1868, Provincetown had fifty-three whaling ships and ninety-one cod fishing boats. There were sometimes as many as six hundred ships in the harbor.

1865 Provincetown's population was 3,475. Most residents were Yankee descendants of English settlers; there were 245 Portuguese immigrants, almost all of them from the Azores; 116 were from Ireland, and 185 were from Cape Breton.

1873 The first passenger train arrived in Provincetown.

1899 Charles Hawthorne started the Cape Cod School of Art, helping to establish the country's oldest continuous art colony.

1907 The cornerstone was laid for the Pilgrim Monument in a ceremony attended by President Teddy Roosevelt.

1915 The Provincetown Players produced their first plays, marking what many consider the birth of modern theater in America.

1921 The last Provincetown-owned whaling ship, the *Charles W. Morgan,* completed its final voyage.

1947 Provincetown celebrated its first Blessing of the Fleet.

1961 The Cape Cod National Seashore was established.

2000 Provincetown's year-round population of about 3,400 is almost identical to what it was in the 1860s, but the population now swells to between 35,000 and 40,000 at the height of summer, with 80,000 to 100,000 crowding into town for special events like the Fourth of July.

1620

*To get to shore, the Pilgrims had to wade through
the bitter-cold water in the pouring rain.*

❖

THEY CAME HERE FIRST

Although many textbooks ignore the fact, good students of Provincetown history know that Plymouth is the second spot the Pilgrims found in the New World. The designation "first landing of the Pilgrims," in fact, belongs to Provincetown. It was here that the *Mayflower* first docked on November 11, 1620 (November 21 according to the modern calendar), about five weeks before the Pilgrims got to Plymouth.

However, it is only fair to state that the tip of Cape Cod was never the Pilgrims' destination. They left Plymouth, England, in early September of 1620, armed with papers to start a new settlement in the Virginia Colony, which at that time extended as far north as today's New York State. They were headed for the Hudson River, but blew off course—by several hundred miles. Using maps made by earlier explorers, including one published in 1616 by Captain John Smith, they sailed in around the tip of Cape Cod, where they found a sheltered harbor.

What they had discovered was not exactly Paradise. According to William Bradford's account: "They had now no friends to wellcome them, nor inns to entertaine or refresh their weatherbeaten bodys, no houses and much less towns to repair too, to seeke for succour. . . . Besids, what could they see but a hidious and desolate wilderness, full of wild beasts and willd men? If they looked behind them, ther was the mightly ocean which they had passed, and was now as a maine barr and goulfe to separate them from all the civill parts of the world."

The first few days did nothing to improve this nightmarish first impression. The Pilgrims had endured sixty-six days onboard the *Mayflower,* only to find that the harbor was too shallow for the boat's draft. So to get to shore, they had to wade through the bitter-cold water in the pouring rain. Many of them took sick, and some died, never having recovered from their first walk to shore.

But at least they had finally arrived somewhere. One of their first tasks was to try to establish order for the group. Since their papers from King James were valid only for the Virginia Colony, they drew up a new set of papers, which they called the Mayflower Compact. In that document, they established the rule of law for the new land and pledged to "combine our selves togeather into a civill body politick, for our better ordering and preservation and furtherance of the ends aforesaid; and by vertue hereof to enacte, constitute and frame shuch just and equall lawes, ordinances, acts, constitutions, and offices, from time to time, as shall be thought most meete and convenient for the generall good of the Colonie, unto which we promise all due submission and obedience."

After a few days, the men set off on small expeditions, during which they occasionally spotted and chased Indians, never quite catching up to them. They found signs of abandoned settlements, often those of Indians who had died of diseases brought over by earlier European explorers. One site had the remains of a house, a European ship's kettle, and a mound of newly dug up land. The men dug it up again and found a basket filled with red, yellow, and blue corn. They took the kettle and the Indians' stash of corn—as much of it as they could carry, anyway—and reburied the rest, on the spot that is now known as Corn Hill in Truro.

They came on deep valleys and a freshwater spring (probably Pilgrim Spring near High Head in North Truro), and plenty of wildlife suitable for hunting: deer, partridges, and flocks of wild geese and ducks. Other people, it appeared, were already taking advantage of this abundance; one night the newcomers spotted a crude deer trap, made with rope and a noose. William Bradford found it first, or rather, it found him, and took him up by the leg.

After a few weeks of exploring, the Pilgrims met to decide whether or not they should stay. On the plus side there were good fishing and whaling (they could see whales in the harbor, though they lacked the harpoons to kill them), and an ample supply of corn. The excellent harbor would be easy to defend, and frankly, they felt that it was just too cold and late in the season to go any farther. On the other hand, there was some worry that the ponds might go dry in hot weather, and, more important, they knew from their maps that there was another harbor directly across the bay; Robert Coppin, the *Mayflower's* pilot, had even been there once. The group divided up; ten headed west across the bay, while the rest stayed on.

During the time the boat was away, both life and death came to the Pilgrims who had waited at the tip of Cape Cod. Peregrine White, the first new "native" Cape Codder, was born, and William Bradford's wife, Dorothy, fell overboard and drowned in the harbor. Nearly 250 years later, an 1869 *Harper's* magazine article, "William Bradford's Love Life," suggested her death might have been, not an accident, but suicide; this version has gained favor as alternative Pilgrim history in some quarters. The writer of the *Harper's* article later admitted that her account was highly imaginative, and that she had taken some degree of poetic license in it, suggesting "rather what 'might have been,' than what is known to have been."

Meanwhile, the explorers on their westward journey found their way to Plymouth, though Plymouth Rock is mere mineral matter; no one is quite sure where the Pilgrims went ashore there. Still, they found a good harbor, excellent topsoil, lots of fish and shellfish, freshwater brooks, and fields that had already been cleared for planting corn. The rest, as they say, is history, at least as most of the world outside Provincetown has come to know it.

EIGHTEENTH CENTURY

THE EIGHTEENTH CENTURY

An early map of Provincetown shows a set of upside-down Vs, just south of what is now Herring Cove Beach. The Vs stand for a set of shacks and lean-tos that fishermen built, so they would be close to good fishing grounds off that stretch of coast. When they finished fishing, they knocked down the structures, or left them to the wind and winter storms. The map marked that spot "Helltown," where the conditions were harsh and the work was dangerous. For some, this moniker took on a slightly different meaning; they used it to describe Provincetown as a whole—a place with mediocre soil that more traditional settlers skipped, a place frequented by English, French, and Portuguese fishermen and whalers, privateers and smugglers. They generally stayed only when the fishing and the weather were good, supplementing work with heavy drinking, brawling, gambling, and other bacchanalian pursuits. A more permanent settlement slowly developed, helped by excellent inshore fishing and whaling. The town's population expanded and contracted like a bellows, especially during wartime, when men would often be captured when they ventured offshore. But with the end of the Revolutionary War, the settlement at land's end took firmer root, and there were over eight hundred residents by 1800. Provincetown built a church, held town meetings, and adopted other marks of civility, if never quite leaving behind its reputation as a place where anything goes.

❖

HELLTOWN

Over the years, there were steady attempts to tame the place with a reputation as "Helltown." In 1714, the Province of Massachusetts established the scruffy gathering place at the tip of the Cape as a precinct under Truro. They called it "Cape Cod," a name Englishman Bartholomew Gosnold first gave the area in 1602, when he found the waters offshore swirling with codfish. Cape Cod included the Province Lands, and it was separated from Truro by a boundary line that ran from "the jaw-bone of a whale set in the ground by the side of a red oak stump" to "a marked pine-tree, standing by a reedy pond." This line would have run roughly along what is now Howland Street, which means that most of today's East End was originally part of Truro. That town boundary was moved further east in the nineteenth century.

Perhaps the legislators thought this new boundary would give definition and order to the rowdy group of settlers at the Cape-tip, but it seems to have had the opposite effect. They ignored the colonial regulations—sold liquor to Indians, refused to get a minister when the previous one left—and considered themselves unencumbered by Truro law. After all, they were a separate precinct, weren't they?

This put Truro in the awkward position of having an unruly ward over which it had no control. What was worse, those people breaking the law always seemed to be having such a good time. In 1715, within a year of the new designation, Truro was sending petitions to the General Court, "praying that Cape Cod be declared a part of Truro or not a part of Truro, that the town may know how to act in regard to some persons."

More than a decade passed before Truro was finally released from its annoying responsibility without jurisdiction. In 1727, the precinct of Cape Cod petitioned the General Court and was granted incorporation as a township. The residents wanted it to be called "Herrington," after the plentiful herring supplies, but the legislators chose "Provincetown." By doing so, the government signified that it would retain control of the Province Lands. The legislation allowed settlers to build on the land, making sure "that no person or persons, be hindered and obstructed in building such wharves, stages, working houses, and flakes, and other things, as shall be necessary for the salting, keeping, and packing their fish, or in cutting down and taking such trees and other materials, growing on said Province lands." However, it also dictated that the land "be held as common as heretofore." In other words, the residents remained squatters, and land could only be sold by quit-claim deed, a legal arrangement that left an owner with no clear title.

Provincetowners continued to live as squatters for the next 165 years, buying and selling property as if it were their own. Several times in the 1880s they petitioned the state legislature to turn over a portion of the Province Lands to the town, but the legislature rejected their request each time. It wasn't until 1893 that Massachusetts finally ceded the land along the harbor to the town, and granted deeds for houses where some families had already been living for over one hundred years. That narrow three-mile strip became Provincetown as it essentially still exists today.

But over two centuries of squatting had its effect on the town's collective psyche. Provincetown has kept its earliest reputation as a maverick port with an attitude of living slightly outside the law, a refuge for the unusual—whether it's artists sandblasting an entire car, men sporting leather caps and pierced nipples, lesbians flaunting stereotype with long hair and lipstick, middle-aged transvestites in Chanel matched separates, or a town manager attired in suitcoat and madras shorts.

And to this day, the rest of the towns on the Cape, like the early Truro, prefer to remain slightly separate from this place, even as their residents like to venture to Land's End, if only for a small taste of its attractions.

❖

MOONCUSSERS

Everybody loves a good find, especially something carried in by the tide and deposited on the beach, free for the taking, like the perfectly preserved lobster pot or buoy that is dragged home for ornamental purposes. And the chances of finding treasures increase dramatically just after a storm.

In a place famous for its shipwrecks—along this stretch of the Atlantic coast, there have been about three thousand wrecks in recorded history—it's not surprising that beachcombing would become a profession. Historian Henry Kittridge thought there was little difference between the idle beachcomber and the professional wrecker. "Differences in motive there may be, of course," wrote Kittredge, "and varying degrees of devotion to the business, but the beachcomber who walks the shores of the Cape on the chance of finding a sound plank or a good piece of rope or a lobster pot or a spar is of the same ilk as the wrecker who hurries to the beach before daylight of a winter's morning at the first news of a wreck, to see what of her cargo or her gear he can get for himself."

A wrecker could make a decent living hauling off whatever washed up from a shipwreck, especially lumber, which was in short supply at the tip of the Cape. Salvage work could be so lucrative, in fact, that some people appeared to prefer it to saving ships. When Ralph Waldo Emerson visited the Cape in 1853, the Nauset Light keeper told him there had been great opposition to the prospect of building the lighthouse, "as it would injure the wrecking business."

This is not to say that wreckers *wanted* the ships to wreck. The only people who would wish for such a thing were the fabled and evil mooncussers, who carried a lantern out to the ocean at night, fixed it to a pole and waved it in the dark along a particularly dangerous stretch of beach. A ship would mistake the lantern for the beam of a lighthouse and head in toward safety, only to wreck on the sandbars and wash up on the beach, where the waiting men would grab its treasures. If the crew members survived the wreck, they'd be murdered so the mooncussers could continue gathering their haul. "Don't get ashore on the back side of Truro," wary Provincetowners warned. "There's a woman there waiting for you with a brick in a stocking." The mooncussers were so named because they would curse whenever the moon appeared, since it gave the ships enough light by which to steer safely.

The only trouble with this story is, there is no record of anyone actually luring boats to shore, or looting one before trying to save the crew onboard. On the other hand, there were plenty of instances of ransacking once the crew was on land—or, in sadder cases, once all onboard had drowned. At that point the goods were free for the taking. Plenty of local cottages have a floor constructed from the galley of a long-lost wreck or a figurehead hanging from a wall.

But the myth of the mooncusser has lasted for centuries. It has a nice, edgy ring, like a good ghost story to be told late at night around a fire.

❖

SAND TAKING OVER PROVINCETOWN

A few years ago, the Cape Cod National Seashore started up a program to plant beach grass to control dune erosion in the Province Lands. It was as though the government had decided to fill the Grand Canyon, so many people protested they should "leave nature alone" and preserve the bare, Sahara-like stretch of sand dunes that blow across Route 6 as you pass Pilgrim Lake, heading into Provincetown.

The irony is that the dunes are as man-made as Route 6 itself. When the Pilgrims arrived here in 1620, the entire area was heavily forested. *Mourt's Relation* (an account of the Pilgrims' early settlement, published in 1622) describes this newly discovered landscape as "all wooded with oaks, pines, sassafras, juniper, birch, holly, some ash, walnut, the wood for the most part open and without underwood, fit to go or ride in." The harbor extended across what is now Beach Point to a second, smaller harbor further inland, called East Harbor, which was separated from the greater Provincetown Harbor by a narrow strip of beach and marsh.

It was only with the permanent settling of Provincetown in 1680 that the landscape we now think of as "natural" began to emerge. But the sandy, open views that seem so emblematic of Provincetown were less a result of aesthetic choice than of the early settlers' lack of planning or conservation principles. They chopped down trees to build houses, boats, and furniture and to provide heat; a typical household could easily burn thirty cords of wood in a single winter. Within a few decades the hillsides were stripped, and the cows were turned loose to graze on whatever scrub vegetation was left.

The result was that sand blew across the dunes and toward town, filling the sky in every strong wind. There was so much erosion that in 1714 the colonial government passed an act to preserve the trees on the dunes (even though the same body gave Provincetowners the right to cut down trees when it granted incorporation in 1727), and in 1739 another law was passed forbidding the grazing of cattle in the dunes.

But what did anyone in Provincetown ever care for laws? Early on, Provincetowners established a tradition of waiting for impending disaster before they would mend their ways. People kept cutting wood and grazing their cows for another hundred years, until East Harbor filled with so much sand it started turning to silt, and a few houses disappeared up to their rooftops. In 1825, when a special government commission released a report showing that the sand was advancing toward the town at a rate of 50 rods, or 825 feet, a year, people finally began to see visions of a sandstorm burying the entire town. They stopped cutting any young pines, kept their cattle penned up, and planted beach grass to stabilize the dunes.

These conservation measures slowed further erosion, but the local cows lost one of their main sources of food. However, like the town's human residents, they too proved to be highly adaptable.

*Fish turned out to be even more to the cows' liking than
the dune grass, so much so that the animals started rushing
to the beach when the fishing boats came in.*

Provincetown's cows eventually made it into the *U.S. Fish Commission Bulletin*, which reported in 1881 that, since the cows were no longer allowed to graze on the dunes, their owners had taught them to eat fish, by adding it to their fodder. Fish turned out to be even more to the cows' liking than the dune grass, so much so that the animals started rushing to the beach when the fishing boats came in. As the fishermen cleaned their catch, the cows would munch away quite happily on the discarded heads and entrails.

Even with these conservation measures, the damage to East Harbor was hard to control. People worried that the delicate beach and marsh between the two harbors could be wiped out in a big storm, opening the way for tons of sand to flow into the main harbor. In 1869 a 1,400-foot-long dike was built to completely separate the two, blocking not only the flow of sand, but any tidal flow as well. East Harbor became Pilgrim Lake. The dike was widened a few years later to become the railroad bed in 1873, and in the 1950s it became the Beach Point section of the new Route 6.

Despite these precautions, trees never did grow back to any extent in the dunes. Patchy stands of pitch pine and scrub oak, cranberry bogs, and compass grass are pretty much all that hold the dunes together. On a windy winter day the sand still blows across the dunes with such force that it sandblasts the windshield of any car that drives along Route 6. Perhaps it is that wildness we cherish most, even if it is partly man-made.

HE SHOULD HAVE STAYED HOME

Even after the Revolutionary War started, many people in the colonies still had Old World sympathies to King George. There was a large exodus from New England for the more sympathetic Nova Scotia, where the word "Tory" could still be uttered with pride.

One Boston Tory, a shopkeeper named Jolly Allen, chartered a sloop called the *Sally*, complete with captain, to transport him, with his wife and possessions, up to Halifax in March 1776. Unfortunately, the *Sally's* captain understood almost nothing about sailing—he didn't even know how to take in the sails. He chose to sail by way of Cape Cod, heading right toward a particularly treacherous stretch of the Atlantic just north of Provincetown. The Peaked Hill Bars are a series of sandbars just offshore that run parallel to the beach. They have caused so many wrecks over the centuries that this length of coast earned the nickname "graveyard of the Atlantic." If a captain wasn't familiar with the area, he could sail the boat too close to shore and get pushed over the outside sandbar by strong winds. Then the boat would be smashed back and forth against the inner and outer bars till it broke into pieces, often within sight of shore.

The *Sally* quickly joined the list of ships wrecked off Peaked Hill. Not only was the boat ruined, but one of its passengers had come down with smallpox. News of the wreck reached Provincetown, and a few men who had already had smallpox, and were therefore immune, rowed out to bring the passengers of the wrecked boat ashore.

Any gratitude Jolly Allen felt for this rescue soon dissipated. He and his wife were carted off to town and held in a squalid little room, where his wife fell ill and eventually died.

The Provincetown selectmen wrote to the Massachusetts Provincial Congress to find out what they should do with the remains of the boat and the rescued Tory sympathizers. Meanwhile, the local wreckers took over salvage operations of the *Sally*. Their job was to remove the cargo and haul it to town to save it for the colonial authorities, but, curiously, almost everything vanished somewhere along the mile-long trek through the sand dunes between Peaked Hill and town.

To make matters even worse, several people visited Jolly Allen to boast about what had become of his possessions. Allen wrote of one such visit, "About fifteen or sixteen men and women was fighting battle royal in the fields, and condemning one another, and each saying the other had taken more of my property than they."

Allen tried an appeal for sympathy by telling his visitors how he had been swindled by the captain, who, after all, didn't know a thing about sailing. He was successful in one sense: they took up his cause, saying a freshwater captain like the one who had sailed the *Sally* should be hanged.

Their goodwill did not, however, help Jolly Allen recover his possessions. By the end of his stay in Provincetown, he had lost his wife, his chartered boat, and all his belongings. He gave up on his plans for Nova Scotia and moved to Watertown instead.

As for the townspeople of Provincetown, they exhibited true chutzpah. After completely stripping and looting the *Sally*, they then turned around and sent a bill to the provisional government for 150 pounds—their fee for saving and hauling the cargo.

No Dogs in Church, No Methodists in Town

Despite Provincetown's long-standing reputation for lawlessness, the town did get religion, albeit slowly. While most New England villages established churches to serve as the center of their communities, Provincetown's first settlers made no moves to build a church. The early itinerant minister preached where he could and did not stay in town long.

A meetinghouse was finally built in the early 1720s and served both church and state. At town meeting, which was held there, men decided church matters as well as municipal ones. Voters approved a salary for the minister in 1773 and bought a Bible with town funds in 1784. Five years later, they okayed the expenditure of two dollars to pay the keeper of the meetinghouse "to swepe it every four weeks and shet and open the winder shetters all the year round."

Town meeting was not limited to church fiscal matters. In 1773, voters decided "that any purson should be found getting cranberys before ye twentyth of September exceding one quart should be liable to pay one doler and have the berys taken away." The dollar fine and the confiscated cranberries went to "they who shall find any pursons so gathering." And in 1775, the town voted that the owners of dogs who wandered into the meetinghouse during services would have to pay a fine of fifty cents, or kill their dogs.

The lack of separation between church and state was especially obvious when the town refused to allow a Methodist church to be built in 1795. But this didn't stop the Methodists. They persevered and built their own church, under great duress, including an attack by a group of Congregational followers, who built a bonfire out of the lumber for the new church and burned an effigy of the Methodist minister on top.

The Methodists fought back with small guerrilla actions; a Methodist selectman stole the key to the meetinghouse and locked out the congregation when members showed up for a meeting. And when the Congregational church's bass viol player became a Methodist, not only did he leave the church; he also took its bass viol with him, figuring that it too had converted.

❖

THE WRECK OF THE *SOMERSET*

The British warship *Somerset* took part in several of the episodes that are now part of Revolutionary War history. During the Battle of Bunker Hill, the *Somerset* protected British soldiers, and Paul Revere had to row past it as he left the Old North Church before climbing on his horse and galloping toward Concord and Lexington to sound the alarm. "A huge black hulk, that was magnified by its own reflection in the tide," wrote Henry Wadsworth Longfellow, describing the ship in his poem "The Midnight Ride of Paul Revere."

Provincetown was nearly abandoned during the Revolutionary War. Because fishermen could be captured by British ships when they ventured offshore, many of them emigrated off-Cape to places where it was still safe to fish.

Many local histories tell how the *Somerset* stayed in Provincetown Harbor during the war, its soldiers rowing in to requisition eggs and butter and charm the local girls. A book about the *Somerset* by Marjorie Hubbell Gibson disputes this, saying the ship's log shows it was never in Provincetown. What is uncontested, though, is that Provincetown is where the ship ended its naval career. On November 2, 1778, the *Somerset* wrecked on the Peaked Hill Bars. The crew tossed guns and supplies overboard to try to lighten the ship's load. Some drowned when waves smashed into their lifeboats, tossing the men overboard. Eventually the waves lifted the *Somerset* off the sandbars and carried it to shore with the remaining crew still alive.

By that point the few local men who were still living in the area had made their way out to the back shore. The British soldiers who had survived, perhaps as many as 450, were arrested and put under guard by the same men who had arrived to help in case the British needed rescuing. Some of the local men acted as escorts and marched the captured British soldiers by foot 120 miles to Boston (although the *Somerset*'s officers were allowed to arrive for their imprisonment via a pleasant sail across Cape Cod Bay). Those local men who were not acting as guards stayed behind to strip anything valuable off the *Somerset*.

The upper portion of the ship's hull was burned on the beach, while the lower half slowly sank deeper and deeper into the sand, until eventually it was completely buried. Like Brigadoon, the wreck of the *Somerset* reappears about once every hundred years. It was uncovered during a storm in 1886 and again in 1973. Each time people appeared with saws and hammers and carried home oak timbers they later carved into ship models, canes, and other souvenirs. After each reappearance, the remaining timbers have shrunk away a little more, poking out like skeleton bones. If the ship keeps to its historical schedule, it should resurface sometime after 2060.

NINETEENTH CENTURY

THE NINETEENTH CENTURY

Provincetown began the nineteenth century as an outpost in the hinterlands, without a road, a sidewalk, or a wharf. But with the development of the salt-making, whaling, and fishing industries, the town slowly began to prosper. Windmills lined the beach, pumping seawater into the salt works' wooden vats. The water would evaporate, leaving behind the salt.

Wharves jutted out into the harbor so fishermen could land vast catches of mackerel and cod. Boats from everywhere flocked to Provincetown, crowding into the harbor. And the first Portuguese men, mostly from the Azores, joined up as extra hands on fishing and whaling boats. Still, the town had to keep finding new ways to continue to prosper to keep up in a quickly changing world. Salt mines were discovered in New York State, providing cheaper and more plentiful salt. Oil was discovered in Pennsylvania, and low-cost kerosene replaced whale oil as fuel for lamps.

When the railroad finally reached Provincetown in 1873, not only did local fishermen gain access to larger markets, but Provincetown saw the beginnings of a whole new industry: tourism. Residents built cottages and hung out a shingle: ROOMS FOR RENT. And in the final year of the century, Charles Hawthorne opened his Cape Cod School of Art, beginning Provincetown's next incarnation, as art colony.

Not Walking the Plank

Before the 1830s there weren't any streets in Provincetown. It was not that the town was too small to need roads—by 1829 the population was already a booming 1,800. But as historian Shebnah Rich noted, "Every man had a path from his house to his boat or vessel, and once launched, he was on the broad highway of nations without tax or toll." What, therefore, was the point of a road? The houses faced the water, the beach was the main drag, and the only navigation was by boat. Rich said one Provincetown boy, seeing a carriage for the first time, "wondered how she could steer so straight without a rudder."

The proposal for constructing the town's first road met with fierce opposition. "We always got along fine without one before," went the thinking. "Why would we want to spend money on that?" There was a new doctor in town with some dreams of grandeur, who proposed a sixty-four-foot-wide boulevard, his version of the Champs Elysées, *sur la plage.* But his idea was shot down as being slightly impractical for a town with no wagon, cart, or oxen, and only a single, one-eyed old white horse, owned by the minister.

Instead, in 1835 the town settled on a twenty-two-foot-wide street, at a cost of $1,273. This width was just broad enough for two carriages to pass each other. Still it wasn't easy to clear enough room to fit the road; the town had to take down or move several houses, salt works, stores, and fish flakes that stood in the way. Some homes sat close to the water and were simply turned around so their front doors would face onto the new street, though the house that now holds the Martin House Restaurant kept its back turned; if you walk down to the beach, you can see that the front door still faces the water. Many of the houses on Commercial Street were moved to their current spots, or built after the street was constructed. Carriages were eventually replaced by cars, and

The sidewalk protestors stubbornly trudged along, walking beside but never on *the sidewalk, hopping over the wooden planks when they needed to get across.*

the dirt road was paved, but Commercial Street has remained the same width of twenty-two feet.

Once the road was built, people started talking about how nice it would be to have a little wooden sidewalk. Opposition was bitter again, especially from some of the older women in town, who swore they would never set foot on the sidewalk as long as they lived. But the sidewalk was approved, and built in 1838, thanks in part to some unexpected funds that the town received, courtesy of a surplus in the federal budget.

Many of the sidewalk protesters kept their word. They stubbornly trudged along, walking beside but never *on* the sidewalk, hopping over the wooden planks when they needed to get across. Some perfected the art of flipping the sand out of their shoes with each step. However, Rich says that in some of the old pictures "the people are represented without feet, it being understood so much was covered by the sand."

❖

CHIP HILL

There is a stone wall under a house in the West End, at the corner of Tremont and Cottage Streets, and the mystery surrounding it has continued for 150 years. The house is built on a spot known as Chip Hill. The story is that the hill was leveled in 1805 and covered with wood chips from a neighbor's woodworking yard, where he built spars for ships (that is where the name, Chip Hill, evidently comes from). The town's salt-making industry was taking off at the time, so they flattened out this piece of land to build a new salt works there. The salt works consisted of low wooden vats used to hold saltwater, which was pumped in by windmill power. The saltwater evaporated in the sun, leaving behind the salt. By the late 1830s, Provincetown had seventy-eight salt works and manufactured almost fifty thousand bushels of salt per year.

When salt mines were discovered in New York State in the late 1840s, the demand for salt from the Cape dropped off quickly, since the process of evaporating saltwater was much more time-consuming and expensive than mining. The salt works around town were torn down, or converted into houses.

On the site of the Chip Hill salt works, when workers dug down to make a cellar for a new house in 1853, they found an old stone and mortar wall already there. The rocks didn't look like anything from around the Cape; they were red, with long black stripes, as if they'd been burned in a fire, and there were ancient-looking fish bones pressed into the mortar.

The discovery of these unfamiliar rocks just happened to follow the publication, a few years earlier, of a history of the Vikings' landing at the tip of Cape Cod. A Danish historian named Carl Christian Rafn brought out his account in 1837, in which he claimed that Thorwald Eriksson—brother of Leif and son of Eric the Red—had landed on the Cape around 1004, so the crew could repair the damaged keel of their boat. They sailed on from there, but soon they encountered Indians, and Thorwald was shot through the armpit by an arrow. It was a mortal wound, but before he died, Thorwald ordered his men to bury him at the spot where they had fixed the ship.

People in town fit this story together with the rocks that seemed from someplace far away, and the old, crumbling mortar, and decided that these rocks had been part of the ballast from Thorwald's boat, and that the wall was, in fact, part of a fort the Vikings had built to protect themselves from the Indians. So the wall became known as the Norsemen's Fort, or the Norsemen's Fireplace, and the legend has lasted ever since.

They incorporated the wall into the cellar of the house built in 1853, which still stands on the corner of Tremont and Cottage. If you go down to the crawl space, you can see the old stone and mortar wall, and some people will tell you it feels different from just any wall. One of Thorwald's descendants visited the house in the fall of 2000 and said he could feel the Vikings' presence in his hands when he touched the rocks. About the same time, scientists from the Woods Hole Oceanographic Institution carted away several hunks of the wall, with the idea that they could carbon-date the mortar and see if the legend held any weight.

Their initial findings were inconclusive, but leaned heavily toward the pedestrian: the mortar appeared to be from the nineteenth century, when the original salt works was built.

True believers can take comfort in the idea that there might be other findings, and, after all, this was only the date of the mortar. Who's to say the rocks themselves did not come from the coast of Iceland or Greenland eight hundred years before? And if the rocks turn out to be from, say, Gloucester, will their power begin to disappear? Like many legends, this one would like to be solved, and also wants to stay untouched.

❖

TELLING THE LOCALS APART

In Provincetown's early days, the town was made up of relatively few families, many of whom shared the same last name. Town records were full of Nickersons and Mayos, Atkinses and Atwoods, Princes and Dyers, and Cooks and Snows. And since many people named their children after an older relative, this led to inevitable confusion; there would be half a dozen Sally Nickersons or Solomon Cooks.

If there were too many Elizabeth Smalls, it was easy enough to differentiate among them as Elizabeth, Beth, Betsy, and Lizzie, but what did one do with seven Phoebes or Esthers?

Residents came up with various systems. For instance, people took to telling the married Esthers apart by adding on a husband's first name, so there was Esther James and Esther Frank, Esther John, and Esther Walter.

Another approach was to call a person by his or her first and middle names and leave off the last name altogether. Let's say you had several children around, all of whom were named Benjamin Atkins or Mary Snow. There would be a Benjamin Elisha and a Benjamin Francis, a Mary Hannah and a Mary Nancy. This practice made a lot of sense within a family or around the neighborhood. But it was very confusing for other people, especially if they were trying to keep track of which brother and sister came from the same family.

People were also likely to pick up nicknames, especially if they already shared a surname. The Portuguese fisherman with a knack for getting cod became Manuel Codfish, and his family therefore was known as the Codfishes. The more descriptive the name, the better it stuck, till most people couldn't even remember the original name. No doubt the woman who became Mrs. Jazzgarters kept her newfound surname long past the end of the Roaring Twenties.

❖

MOUNT ARARAT AND MOUNT GILBOA

The dunes of the Province Lands recall the hilly, desertlike landscape of the Old Testament Holy Land. By the early nineteenth century, students of the Bible had dubbed two of the highest peaks, which face each other across modern-day Route 6 at the Provincetown-Truro line, as Mount Ararat and Mount Gilboa.

The original Mount Ararat, in Turkey, is the spot where Noah is said to have moored his ark after the flood. To honor Noah as the world's first successful sailor, local seamen christened the mountain's namesake here. The local Mount Gilboa is named after a biblical mountain that overlooks the Mediterranean, and which appears in the book of Samuel. David, lamenting the death of King Saul and his son on Mount Gilboa during a battle with the Philistines, calls out, "Ye mountains of Gilboa, let there be no dew or rain upon you nor upsurging of the deep." David's quote conjures up the storms and heavy seas fisherman might encounter in any trip off Provincetown.

Mount Gilboa has been put to several practical, as well as biblical, uses over the years. It holds the radio antenna for WOMR, Provincetown's community radio station, as well as one of the town's water storage tanks. In 1989 someone came up with a plan to spruce up the water tower by painting life-sized whales on its side. After some discussion, however, the townspeople declined a visual rendition of the "upsurging of the deep."

FLOATING HOUSES

Like many places around Cape Cod, Provincetown had a long tradition of moving houses from one spot for another. Since all the town's land legally belonged to the state until the 1890s, people were really only buying and selling the houses they had built on state land. And since one neighbor didn't own the land anymore than another did, it was easy enough to haul a house to a more attractive site.

A whole neighborhood moved in the 1850s and 1860s, when the entire settlement at Long Point floated, house by house, across Provincetown Harbor. Long Point is the narrow spit of land that curls around to form the very tip of the Cape. In 1818, the first building went up there, and by the late 1840s, a little mirror town faced Provincetown across the harbor. It had two hundred people, thirty-eight houses, a schoolhouse, and a store, with six windmills to pump seawater and make salt, a wharf, and a tryworks to render whale blubber.

The settlement broke up for various reasons. Many of the people moved there originally to get faster access to the fishing grounds in the bay. But as fish migrated to other areas, there was no longer any great advantage in living out on Long Point. The Point was also so narrow and delicate, people were afraid that storms would wash it away altogether. Most of the houses were moved across the harbor in the 1850s, and the last one left in 1867. The houses floated across on big flat-bottomed scows—so gently, so the story goes, that the cooking stoves stayed lit throughout the move, and the women went right on fixing dinner.

*A whole neighborhood moved in the 1850s and 1860s,
when the entire settlement of Long Point floated,
house by house, across Provincetown Harbor.*

You can still spot Long Point's floating houses around town, especially along Commercial Street in the West End. Each one is identified by a small blue-and-white ceramic plaque that shows a house on a barge and the Long Point lighthouse in the background.

Long Point itself stayed put, even gaining temporary armaments: two sand embankments with cannons were built in 1864 to defend Provincetown during the Civil War. These weapons, it should be said, were never used, and were dubbed Fort Useless and Fort Ridiculous.

Nonetheless, worries about the waves breaking through the slender spit of land never went away. In 1911, the federal government built a breakwater out of about 1,200 blocks of Rockport granite, starting at the Provincetown Inn and running just over a mile, out to Wood End. The rocks have settled and fallen and been replaced over the decades, but the basic structure remains, forming a sort of teetering bridge of piled-up rocks you can pick your way across to Long Point. It is best to time such a walk with the time of the month and the pull of the moon, lest you be swept off the rocks during a particularly high tide.

❖

LOST LAUNDRY

When the English steamship *Caledonia* wrecked near Race Point on New Year's Day, 1863, it delivered a dressmaker's dream to those on shore; Irish linen, cotton, and wool came bobbing in on the waves. Herman Jennings tells of one man who rescued an entire bolt of linen toweling as a gift for his wife. It was stained from the saltwater, so she washed it, but where to let it dry? If she hung it outside, everyone would know she had stolen it from the wreck. Craftily, she used her neighbor's clothesline, which butted up against hers.

The plan backfired. Her neighbor apparently thought, if I'm going to suffer the slings and arrows of gossip, I might as well

*The whale, with its mouth gaping open, headed directly
for the boat and crashed into the side.*

enjoy the spoils too—and took in the clean laundry. What was the "actual" owner to do? She couldn't very well knock on her neighbor's door and say, "Excuse me, did you happen to take the linen towels my husband stole off the *Caledonia*?" Neither neighbor mentioned it again, nor did they talk of anything else, for they were no longer on speaking terms after the incident.

❖

THE VOYAGE OF THE *ALCYONE*

Although New Bedford became the center of whaling by the end of the nineteenth century, that town's whalers learned everything they knew from Nantucket whalers. And those on Nantucket learned their craft from the men of Provincetown and other parts of the Cape.

The fastest and easiest means of catching whales was to use the inshore method, which essentially consisted of being at the right place at the right time—during a stranding. Records dating back four hundred years show that schools of pilot whales (called "blackfish" because of their shiny black bodies) have beached themselves periodically along Cape Cod Bay. There are endless theories for this phenomenon, such as a sick pod's committing collective suicide, confusion during a storm, or inner ear problems that muddle the whales' directional signals. Many of the old Cape Codders read strandings as a gift from God. Heeding the proverb "God helps those who help themselves," they learned that they could help nature along by surrounding the churning whales with small boats and beating the water with oars to drive more animals onto the beach. In 1874, during one of the largest recorded strandings, Provincetown men and boys rushed to Truro to help 1,400 whales onto the beach.

Still, the biggest whaling profits came, not through strandings, but from offshore whaling. Vessels made voyages over thousands of miles and dozens of months, journeying around the world to the South Pacific and north to the Arctic Circle. Many of the long-distance whalers came from Provincetown; they had adventuring in their blood.

Whaling was hardly what you'd call glamorous work. Take, for example, one voyage of the *Alcyone*, a 137-ton Provincetown vessel that departed in October 1868 and did not return until June 1871. The crew found a sperm whale off the Gold Coast of Africa, and fired a bomb lance into it. When the whale came back up to the surface and spouted, the *Alcyone* crew saw blood in the salt spray. They figured the whale was dead. Several of them climbed into a whaleboat to move close enough to hit the whale with a hand lance, then haul it back to the *Alcyone*.

The whale, however, was not quite dead. It would be anthropomorphic to claim that the whale was angry at the men and sought revenge. Nonetheless, the whale, with its mouth gaping open, headed directly for the boat and crashed into the side. The unfortunate man holding the lance fell into the mouth. The whale caught the man just below his knees, closed its jaw, and swallowed. Unlike Jonah, the man did not reemerge with a story; rather, what was left of him eventually surfaced, and was recovered and brought back to the *Alcyone*.

This would be enough hardship for any trip, not to mention the requisite storms and other natural disasters. However, later in the voyage, the *Alcyone* was captured by Malay pirates, who took the crew below deck and imprisoned them. The pirates then used the whaling boat as their disguise to get close to other ships in the China Sea, which they robbed and sank.

The pirates eventually abandoned the *Alcyone* on Mauritius, in the Indian Ocean. The boat set out again, but because so many men had been lost to angry whales and pirates, not to mention disease and other causes, the captain, Joseph Baldwin, was forced to stop along the South African coast to recruit enough crew for his return trip to Provincetown. His wife was on the voyage, and he took her along on a visit to a South African tribal chieftain. What transpired was an unexpected lesson in cross-cultural etiquette. Mrs. Baldwin baked some doughnuts and brought them as a little hostess present. Her offering was apparently a hit, for the next day the chief and two others in the tribe paid a return visit to the *Alcyone*. Instead of wearing the usual ceremonial robes, the men arrived naked. Captain Baldwin forced his wife below deck and demanded that she produce three dresses from her steamer trunk, which the chief and his men had to put on before Mrs. Baldwin was allowed back on deck.

LANCY MANSION

It is hard to think of 230 Commercial Street as the grandest house in town. You barely notice it anymore; the basement is now Front Street Restaurant, and the first floor has been turned into a collection of shops selling T-shirts and sunglasses.

But if you look up to the third floor, above the shop fronts, you can still see ornate reminders of a bygone era: the dormers with fretted scrolls, wrought-iron trim around high turrets, and Mediterranean-style tiles on the roof of the former Lancy mansion, built in the French Second Empire style. In the 1870s, Nabby Cook Lancy, the matriarch of her clan, convinced her wealthy merchant son Benjamin to build her a fancy house. But it couldn't be just any fancy house: she wanted a Boston brownstone, which was the fashion at that time. It turned out to be impossible to get the necessary materials to Provincetown, but Benjamin Lancy took this as a challenge. He had the wood for the siding cut to look like stone blocks; then the siding was painted brown and covered with a mixture made out of brownstone sand. And voilà—in 1874, Nabby Lancy got her faux Boston brownstone on Commercial Street, a twenty-room mansion complete with widow's walk, cupola, and water view.

Nabby Lancy got the house she wanted, and even after her death, she went on living there, in a fashion. She died in February 1896, in the heart of the winter, the ground frozen too hard to dig a grave. So the family opened all the windows in her room and propped up the matriarch in bed, where they could visit her each day and pay homage, combing her hair, and occasionally trimming her nails. This went on for weeks, though come spring, the neighbors began to complain, and the family finally had to bury her, but not until May.

There is some confusion about what became of the family and its fortune. According to an oft-repeated version, when Benjamin Lancy died, his son ransacked the house, searching for the secret formula to manufacture faux brownstone, which he figured would make him a fortune. But the son never found anything. He and his sister eventually boarded up the house and moved into the basement, where they lived on the cheap while dreaming of their lost, would-be fortune.

However, historian Clive Driver told a different tale. In his version, Benjamin was well-known for both his miserly and eccentric ways. For instance, he would gather up horse manure left in the streets to burn as fuel and was known to go skinny dipping and then walk home from the beach, still naked, carrying his clothes. After Nabby Lancy's death, he moved down to the basement with his sister, Maria, and lived there for the next twenty-five years.

Perhaps the confusion lies in the name Benjamin Lancy, which, according to Driver, was also the name of Lancy's son, who disappeared with an opera-singing mother early on. When Maria, the sister, died in 1922, the long-lost Benjamin magically reappeared, and had his father Benjamin declared insane and committed to a state hospital. When Benjamin the elder died, the son inherited his money.

Regardless of which version is correct, this much is known for sure. In 1923, the Lancys sold the house to a group of Mayflower descendants called the Research Club, and the mansion became the town's first historical museum. It was then turned over to the Cape Cod Pilgrim Memorial Association, which operates the Monument. When a museum was built next to the Monument in 1961, the association sold off the Lancy mansion to a private buyer.

A DEM BIG SPLESH

There are many events that mark when a place "started to change." For Provincetown, one of those occurred in 1873 when the Old Colony Railroad finished laying its track all the way to the end of the Cape. Less than twenty years earlier, Henry David Thoreau had walked the Outer Beach to Provincetown and found it "a wild, rank place," unlikely to attract the summer tourist. "The time must come when this coast will be a place of resort for those New Englanders who really wish to visit the seaside," Thoreau wrote in *Cape Cod*. "At present it is wholly unknown to the fashionable world, and probably it will never be agreeable to them. If it is merely a ten-pin alley, or a circular railway, or an ocean of mint-julep, that the visitor is in search of—if he thinks more of the wine than the brine, as I suspect some do at Newport—I trust that for a long time he will be disappointed here."

Although the idea of Provincetown as the next Newport was anathema to Thoreau, other people welcomed the prospect. By the end of the Civil War, the town was falling on hard times. Extending the railroad to Provincetown seemed a solution, and the editor of the *Provincetown Advocate* wrote editorials practically every week, boosting the idea. "All those towns through which railroads pass have increased in wealth much more rapidly, since the advent of the iron horse, than those other towns having no railroad facilities," he wrote in 1869. "Quick and cheap locomotion is wealth."

On July 22, 1873, the first train from Boston to Provincetown "united us to the world," as one reporter wrote. Flags and streamers hung from practically every house and boat, and kids walked down the street waving their own miniature versions.

The railroad company had no idea what the response would be. As soon as the train reached the Cape, the cars started filling up, so by the time they got to Orleans, it was standing room only on all thirteen bright yellow coach cars, with people hanging off the platforms. At Wellfleet a few people managed to wedge their way aboard, but that was it—the rest of the way, the train abandoned its scheduled stops, and those onboard just waved down to the people who stood on the platforms, waving back with their flags and handkerchiefs. Every hill in Truro was covered with people in their holiday clothes, whistling and cheering and waving as the train went by.

Donald Trayser recounts that one woman on board was clearly a bit nervous that she was going to miss her destination, as she watched the train hurtling past its Truro stops. She kept pestering the conductor—"Are we almost there? Are you sure the train is going to stop in Provincetown?"—until he finally turned to her and said, "Lady, if it doesn't, der will be a *dem big splesh.*"

You could say the railroad changed everything in Provincetown. Before that, all the fish had to be salted and dried out on flakes along the beach to keep it from spoiling, and then it was shipped out to market by boat. However, once the railroad came, fishermen could sail in, tie up at the wharf, and load their catch straight onto the next train heading out. By the next morning, the catch was in the window of a fish market in Boston or New York, still fresh.

To travel to Provincetown, you didn't have to be an adventurer like Thoreau anymore, trudging through sand for days with a rucksack. From New York, you could take a steamer to Fall River and from there, transfer to a train for the Cape. Visitors from Boston no longer had to contend with stiff headwinds and sea-sickness. They just stepped onto the train in Boston with a little suitcase, and four hours later a porter helped them down onto Railroad Wharf at Provincetown Harbor.

In came the visitors with their hatboxes and gowns. Up went the new guesthouses and summer cottages. After all, people needed someplace to sleep. Provincetown became, for the first time, a destination.

A few people can still remember getting off the train and walking to their hotel with a large trunk loaded for the entire summer. They remember how people called it the "sand train," because the freight cars used to haul sand off the dunes to places off-Cape. Or how the old coal locomotives sometimes sparked brush fires along the route. Or how Dr. Hiebert rode with patients to Boston in the unheated freight cars, before the town had an ambulance.

But beyond memory, there's little left of the "iron horse" that put Provincetown on the map. Once cars and trucks came on the scene, the train business slowed down. Passenger service stopped in 1938, and the last freight train came through in 1960. The railroad ties were taken up and sold as garden timbers, and many were burned in a bonfire celebrating Wellfleet's two hundredth anniversary in 1963, which sent a creosote cloud over neighboring towns. You can still walk sections of the old railroad bed from Wellfleet to Provincetown, but most of the right-of-way got swallowed up as house lots. A long stretch of the old dirt track runs through the woods between Route 6 and 6A, just east of town. There you can still find crumbling, petrified coal cinders buried in the dust.

❖

Fourteen Numbered but Unnamed Graves

It is almost impossible to find it now. You have to go north of town, across Route 6, and take a small footpath near Clapp's Pond. There's no marker or sign showing the way, and the woods are overgrown and tangled. Somehow the air feels slightly colder inside that thicket.

When you get to the site, you will see only a few small, gray weathered stones carved with numbers, but no names. A gully marks the old cellar hole where the Pest House stood.

This is all that's left of the town's smallpox hospital and cemetery. Provincetown had its first outbreak of the highly contagious disease in 1801, and the standard treatment was to keep anybody who had contracted the illness as far away as possible from everyone else. Even though a smallpox vaccine had been developed back in 1796, most people were reluctant to try it. The vaccination wasn't just an injection, like it is now; a person had his skin sliced several times with a knife, then a form of the virus was put into the open wound. People figured, why court death so actively?

To slow down the rate of infection, the town made it illegal for more than six people to get together for "rolicking or any unnecessary purpose." Officials also killed any animals they found wandering away from their houses or pens.

In 1848, the selectmen set aside a piece of land they called the Eastern Plain, and the town built a small house where people with smallpox could be taken care of. The land around the building became the cemetery. Anyone who died was quickly buried, and the clothes and any other belongings were burned. Between 1855 and 1873, Provincetown had fourteen deaths from smallpox. There might have been even more, but in late 1872, the town hired a doctor who had experience handling outbreaks of smallpox. His approach seems to have worked, because the last reported death from smallpox came just a few weeks after the doctor arrived in town. There was one exception: a man who arrived on the Boston boat the following May (who may already have had the disease when he got to Provincetown). In any event, the man's body was buried in the smallpox cemetery nine days later. By late 1873, the board of health declared the town officially smallpox-free.

The fourteen bodies were buried in a semicircle near the Pest House, facing northwest. Now only seven of the stones remain, and the numbers have faded from all but four.

❖

TOWN CRIER

The town crier was, in his day, the principal source of news around town. There was no local newspaper till 1854, and even that was limited to weekly bulletins only a few pages long. The town crier walked up and down the street, shouting out regular news reports to anyone passing by. Late-nineteenth-century town criers George Washington Ready and Walter Smith were known for their ability to spin out even the smallest news item into a delightful symphony of rhetorical excess, whether they were detailing which country in Europe was about to declare another war, where the latest school of cod had been spotted, or how many inches of snow had fallen the night before.

The town crier also supplemented his income by serving as a vehicle for advertising, announcing who needed a couple of extra men to haul in some nets, who had a nice, practically new dory for sale, or which shop had just gotten in a supply of new hats. If an extra coin or two were slipped into his pocket, he would cry even louder or peddle said item a few blocks further through town. He could make a decent living in this fashion, especially during the summer.

The last year-round town crier, Walter Smith, began the job in the 1890s and retired in 1927. With the rise of newspapers and radio, his services were no longer deemed essential. In 1935, the business community saw the post as a way to merge quaint Cape Cod custom with drummed-up tourist business, and the selectmen reestablished the tradition. Former town criers had dressed as they pleased, but the new version appeared in a Pilgrim's outfit, with a high-necked white shirt, buckled shoes, and a wide black hat. He waited on the wharf, greeting the Boston boat as it sailed in, ringing his big brass bell and crying, "Hear ye, Hear ye," calling out the names of guesthouses with vacant rooms, or where to go for lobster dinner.

Provincetown's last town crier, Gene Poyant, hung up his bell when the selectmen refused to renew his contract in 1986, in part because he had made less than flattering remarks about lesbians. He pleaded his case before the voters at town meeting, but they turned down his request for a raise, and the custom of the town crier came to a quiet end.

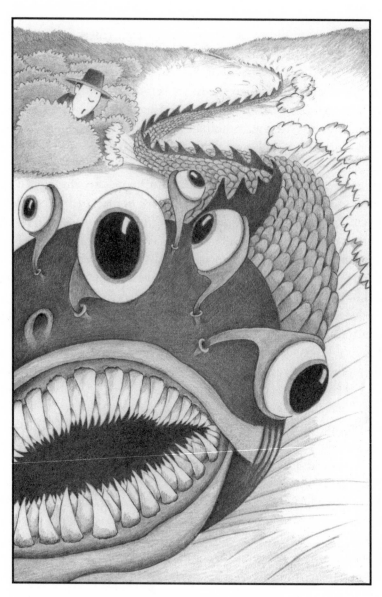

It was, obviously, a sea serpent.

Professor Ready and the Sea Serpent

George Washington Ready, one of Provincetown's town criers with a reputation for embellishment, swore to the following account, which appeared in the Yarmouthport *Cape Cod Item* in 1886.

Mr. Ready—or the "Professor" as he liked to be called—was out for a stroll, when he saw something off Herring Cove Beach, spraying jets of water fifty feet up into the air like a whale. Except that it was longer than a whale—three hundred feet long, to be exact—and covered entirely in red, green, and blue scales. He could see that it had four rows of teeth, two feet long, and an eight-foot-long horn that jutted out from the end of its nose. It also had six eyes (three red and three green, each one the size of a dinner plate). They bounced back and forth on their own tentacles, so the creature could see in all directions at once. It was, obviously, a sea serpent.

Despite the sea serpent's oversized sensory features, it didn't seem to notice Professor Ready when it came up onto the beach and slithered by, a scant thirty feet from where he was crouched down in some beach plum bushes. The serpent slid into the woods, whacking down the oaks and pines in its path like a dragon version of Paul Bunyan, and leaving a sulphurous smell behind.

Professor Ready, like any good detective, tailed it past Clapp's Pond to Pasture Pond. He watched it slide into Pasture Pond. Then, as the serpent disappeared, the water started funneling down into a giant hole in the middle of the pond, like the world's biggest bath going down the drain, leaving behind nothing but a dry pond and a twenty-foot-wide hole.

Should anyone think this was a tall tale, Professor Ready prepared an official affidavit to document his experience. He testified in great detail, adding, for emphasis, "It is a true description of the serpent as he appeared to me on that morning, and I was not unduly excited by liquor or otherwise."

Though he made himself available for interviews, there were few takers.

MESSAGE IN A BOTTLE

The *Monte Tabor* set sail from Sicily on the summer solstice of 1896, carrying salt and eventually bound for Boston. During its North Atlantic crossing, the ship ran into numerous storms, and the constant buffeting appears to have shaken Captain Genero's sense of hope. On September 9, he fashioned a final message, detailing the vessel's position, the size of the waves, and the futility of the crew's efforts to escape the storms. He wrote, in Italian, "The captain and crew, all resigned to the will of Providence, gave their souls to God, thanking him for the destiny assigned to them. Our prayer from the finder for their souls. (signed) The Captain, Genero."

The will of Providence assigned them, however, turned out to be slightly different. The storm must have abated, for though the letter was put into a sealed bottle, it was never tossed overboard. Several days later, as the *Monte Tabor* neared Cape Cod, bad weather returned, and the captain and crew made their way through thick fog, heading for the safety of Provincetown Harbor. The lookout spotted Highland Light blinking from the coast of Truro. This was where they made their mistake; the men mistook the light for Race Point and therefore kept heading west, thinking they would then come around the inside curve of the Cape and into Provincetown Harbor.

Instead, they sailed straight into the graveyard of the Atlantic, the set of offshore sandbars known as the Peaked Hill Bars. The wind was blowing at 40 knots, with hurricane-force gusts, and around midnight the ship stranded offshore between the outer and inner bars. From the beach, the surfmen at the Peaked Hill Life-Saving Station could see the dim outline of the vessel. But the surf was too rough to send out a boat. As they set up their equipment to try to shoot a line onto the *Monte Tabor*, some of the men on shore paced up and down the beach, looking out into the dark. They began to hear cries from the water and then spotted the *Monte Tabor*'s ripped up cabin, separated from the rest of the ship and pitching in the surf close to shore. Several crewmen were clinging to the flotsam, the waves lurching over the side.

The surfmen shouted at the *Monte Tabor* crew to stay put and hold on. Whatever this sounded like, it clearly didn't translate well to the Italian crew. Instead of waiting, one of the men jumped into the water. The surfmen plunged in and pulled him out. Then three more of the Italians jumped, and again, the surfmen managed to haul the battered swimmers to safety. They threw a line to the two Italians who were still hanging onto the cabin. The Italians managed to catch the line, secured it, and were towed close enough to shore that they were able to wade onto the beach.

The next morning, the surfmen on patrol spotted a boy hiding in the beach plum bushes near the beach. The boy started running, as if fleeing the police. They chased him, calling out for him to stop. Eventually they caught him and got enough of his story to understand why he had run. The cabin boy had floated to shore hanging from some of the wreckage. He was hiding so they wouldn't murder him. The older crew members had told him this was the fate of shipwrecked sailors on Cape Cod.

The surfmen continued their patrol and came upon Captain Genero, lying on the beach at the edge of the water. He was dead, but not drowned—his throat was cut. Lying near him was Seaman Biagio; his throat was also cut. Half a mile up the beach, they spotted Olivari, the steward, shot through the head.

The Italian consul was brought in to investigate the deaths, and, with the help of the rescued crew, pieced together an explanation. As the *Monte Tabor* had smashed back and forth between the sandbars and started breaking up, the survivors recounted, Captain Genero embraced each crew member and kissed him on both cheeks. He left them in the cabin, climbed down the ladder to the hold below, and, rather than face the disgrace of being shipwrecked and losing the boat, slit his throat. Biagio followed suit, according to the cabin boy who had witnessed the suicides. A few minutes later the cabin had broken free from the rest of the ship, with the men holding on to it. They had missed Olivari's final moments.

As it turned out, the will of Providence was that, of the crew of twelve on the *Monte Tabor*, six were rescued after the wreck, one floated ashore, three committed suicide, and two bodies were never found. The unsent message, still sealed inside its bottle, was found washed up on the beach near Peaked Hill. It was translated by the Italian consul.

❖

NAMES AND DIRECTIONS

The two long streets that run through town have been known by various names. In its early incarnation, Commercial Street was known as the County Road, and a map from 1870 shows the early Bradford Street as Parallel Street. Around 1874, after Bradford Street was finished, people started calling the County Road "Front Street," since it was in front of the water. Bradford Street, being the street behind it, became "Back Street," and both nicknames have stuck to this day, at least among some residents.

Each end of town also has a name: the East End runs toward Truro, and the West End, toward the breakwater. If you were walking toward the hillier West End, you were said to be heading "up-along," and if you made it all the way to Gull Hill in the far West End, that was "way-up-along." Someone walking toward the East End was going "down-along."

Such cross-town navigating was fairly unusual. Even in such a small town there were distinctions between neighborhoods; for many years people in the West End wouldn't be caught dead moving to the East End, and vice versa. Traditionally, if you were a Yankee, you lived in the East End, and the Portuguese settled in the West End. The Portuguese fishermen might make their way across town, especially visiting the summer ladies staying over in the East End. But the wives and children often never made it past the center of town.

These distinctions have blurred in recent decades, but even now if a couple splits up, instead of leaving town, one can relocate to the opposite end of town, secure in the knowledge that he or she will be unlikely to run into the other.

❖

GHOSTS OF THE PORTLAND GALE

November 27, 1898. It was a freak hurricane, considered one of the major disasters in maritime history. Five hundred people were killed in the Portland Gale, and more than twenty vessels were lost. The storm takes its name from the *Portland*, a steamer that ignored storm warnings and sailed out of Boston over the Thanksgiving holiday in a snowstorm. Headed for Portland, Maine, the vessel carried close to two hundred passengers and crew.

The night after the gale, the first sign of trouble washed up on the back shore, near Peaked Hill: a life preserver with the name of the steamer stamped on one side. Then bodies began to come ashore, from Peaked Hill down to Chatham. But the *Portland* was never found. People assumed the steamer went down near the Peaked Hill Bars, off High Head in North Truro. It would be almost a century before the mystery would be solved. A group from the Historical Maritime Group of New England finally discovered the ship in 1989, ninety-one years after it had disappeared. The *Portland* was nowhere near the Cape, but about twenty miles north, off Cape Ann.

The Portland Gale changed Provincetown Harbor forever. The physical damage from the storm was extraordinary. It destroyed dozens of wharves, the litter of broken pilings lapping against the shoreline. In another age, this kind of destruction would have meant massive rebuilding, but the Portland Gale coincided with a downturn in the fisheries. Both fishing along the Grand Banks and whaling had declined, so there was little financial incentive to rebuild the wharves. A few were replaced, but most of the pilings were simply left to weather in the saltwater and sun, poking out of the sand at low tide like phantom trees.

Josef Berger and others tell the tale of another ghost left in town by the Portland Gale—a Provincetown fisherman named Captain John Santos. Several years earlier, a shark had attacked the captain and eaten his leg. Captain Santos returned home and got a wooden leg that was so beautifully crafted, he carried furniture polish around with him to keep the wood shined.

When the Portland Gale hit, Captain Santos's trawler was ten miles off Race Point. The day after the storm, the surviving crew returned to town in their battered boat and reported that the captain and two other men had been washed overboard. Captain Santos's body was never found, but a few days later, his wooden leg washed up on the beach. The men took it to the captain's widow, Mary. She kept the leg and would talk to it sometimes, as if her husband were still there.

A year later, on the anniversary of the storm, the captain's ghost came to his wife in the night. "We're in for thick weather, and I'll want my store leg to keep me steady when she strikes," he told her. Mary woke, carried the leg out of the cupboard, and left it by the fireplace. That night, there was a terrible storm. The wind was howling, and the rain clattered against the roof. Mary heard this strange *thump thump thump* coming from downstairs, and then what sounded like the front door shutting.

She spent the rest of the night lying in her bed trying not to move. When she finally got up in the morning, she found the leg leaning against the fireplace where she had left it, but it was soaking wet.

The leg got wet from the rain coming down the chimney—that is what she tried to tell herself. But as the day progressed, she fell into more and more of a state, till Dr. Atwood had to be called in to examine her. He couldn't find anything physically wrong with her, but there was clearly something amiss. He kept at her, asking questions, till she finally told him the story.

Dr. Atwood went downstairs, examined the wooden leg, then came back to her bedroom. He told her to have someone take the leg out to sea, weigh it down with leaded nets, and dump it overboard. "I'm a doctor and I don't listen to stories," he told her. "But I put my tongue to that wood. *It don't rain saltwater!*"

❖

OUT WITH THE OLD, IN WITH THE NEW

At the turn of the century, a *Chicago Tribune* reporter visiting Provincetown found quaint local customs that seemed like vestiges of an earlier era: brooms made of halibut fins attached to poles, awnings crafted from stretched porpoise skins, women's hats trimmed with mackerel gills, and clothespins fashioned from little smoked fish so that their mouths snapped over the line. A turtle shell with whalebone handle was used as the church collection plate, and a rope made from knotted eels was pulled to ring the bell.

But signs of the future were in evidence as well. A book published in 1902 ran an ad for Campbell's Livery and Boarding Stable, furnishing drivers "to accompany tourists to the Life-saving stations and all other points of interest." John Adams was selling "fancy" groceries, and the advertisement for the Seashore Estates company in Boston would still seem apropos a century later: "Development, improvement, and care of estates a specialty."

TWENTIETH CENTURY

THE TWENTIETH CENTURY

Over the decades, tourism replaced fishing as Provincetown's mainstay. But the town's twentieth-century story is not only about industry. One of the biggest shifts took place in the first fifteen years of the century, when the mostly Portuguese population—the Picos and Lisbons who emigrated from the Azores and mainland Portugal—made room for a heady mix of painting students, anarchists, and writers from Greenwich Village, and expatriate artists escaping Europe and World War I. Provincetown became one of the most exciting centers of art, literature, and theater in the country. The town's reputation as an art colony has continued to this day, as has its tradition as a place that has made room for people with new ideas and sensibilities: abstract expressionists hosting proto-happenings; long-haired men and women in Army fatigues sleeping on the Meat Rack; gay men and lesbians holding hands on the street; Jamaican immigrants cooking "jerk" chicken at local restaurants.

"Provincetown ain't what it used to be," say the old-timers. "I've never felt so free anyplace," marvel the newcomers. But the charm of the place transcends the arguments. There is something in the narrow streets, with their small white houses and tangled flower gardens, that feels like a European village; something in the pace of Commercial Street on a summer night that's very New York; and something in the hard-edged, brilliant red of a November sunset on the bay that feels like the edge of the world. It's all Provincetown and nowhere else.

❖

THE BIRTH OF AN ART COLONY

Jay Saffron, who was a photographer and NBC cameraman in the 1940s and 1950s, said he had to adjust his cameras by two f-stops when he worked in Provincetown. It seems as if there is always more light here than anywhere else. The sun bounces off the sand and shop windows and white houses, and the water shines and glimmers and echoes off almost every surface. No harbor on the Cape shimmers quite like Provincetown Harbor at the end of the day, the sunset reflecting off the water like a calm pink-gold mirror.

That quality of light is what attracted Charles Hawthorne when he opened his Provincetown painting school—that, and the fact that he was out of a job. Hawthorne was a former student of William Merrit Chase and had been working as Chase's assistant at his summer art school in Southampton, Long Island. Hawthorne thought he might take over the school as Chase got too busy to run it. But instead of stepping down, Chase closed the school, so Hawthorne had to come up with another plan. He looked around on the East Coast for a place that could work as an open-air art school. He was from Maine, and at first he decided on a little town there that he liked. But after visiting Provincetown, he changed his mind.

Hawthorne was primarily a figure painter, and not only did the town offer exquisite light; it had an endless supply of subject matter: the young boy preparing for his first fishing trip; a woman sewing; fishermen hauling up their nets or repairing them by lamplight. The sounds of Portuguese filtered through the town— the Portuguese outnumbered the Yankees by this point—and the narrow, crooked streets with crowded-together houses and flowers spilling over white fences had a European look and feel.

Hawthorne opened his Cape Cod School of Art in Provincetown in 1899. As his reputation grew, the school pulled in more and more students. Provincetown was beautiful and cheap; young women could stay in genteel boardinghouses where

The students would stand before their canvases along the wharf,
in their long white dresses and broad hats, or holding parasols,
looking like the bucolic subject matter for a painting.

a meal cost only twenty cents, and the men could make a studio out of an old fish shed.

Hawthorne pushed his students to understand form through the contrast of shadows and light, bringing them outside to paint in brilliant sunlight. One of his favorite models, the "Mudhead," was a woman who sat in the sun with her face shaded by a wide-brimmed hat or parasol. Instead of being distracted by painting the details of her upturned nose or thin lips, students could focus on contrasting tones and shapes, what Hawthorne called "the beauty of one spot of color coming against another." He liked for them to use putty knives instead of brushes, or even their fingers. "Go out like a savage, as if paint had just been invented," he commanded them.

The students—most of them women—would stand before their canvases along the wharf, in their long white dresses and broad hats, or holding up parasols, looking like the bucolic subject matter for a painting. Hawthorne had always wondered how Chase, his former teacher, could "do as much as he did with all those women togging around," but he didn't seem to mind the droves of adoring females in his classes.

So many students flocked to town that by 1916, there were five separate schools of art advertising for students. Along with Hawthorne's school, students could choose from George Elmer Brown's West End School of Art; a summer painting school with E. Ambrose Webster; the Modern School of Art run by Bror J. O. Nordfeldt, William and Marguerite Zorach, M. Musselman Carr, and Frederick Burt; and George Sensany's classes in color and monochrome etching. Each school had a different philosophy and style, so, for instance, a painter could study Impressionism or post-Impressionism, white-line block printing, or Cubism.

Artists often persuaded local men and women to model for them. One fisherman, probably sitting for a devotee of futurism, was not too happy with the results. "Of course I'm not much on looks now, but you ought to've seen me when they got through with me," he complained.

The conflicts that arose from so many distinct approaches—not to mention the delicate egos and wild temperaments—led to an increasingly heated split between the traditionalists and the modernists. The traditionalists controlled the operations of the Provincetown Art Association, stacking the exhibitions with more representational fare. By 1927, there was so much fighting over who should get wall space at the gallery that the Art Association had to split its schedule. For the next decade, each group had its own show, selected by its own jury.

Eventually animosities mellowed, in part because the lessons of abstract art were starting to seep into more traditional work. Although the two groups kept their separate juries, in 1937 they started to hang works in the same show. The first combined exhibition attracted critics from Boston and New York, and most agreed that the paintings were starting to look alike. The *New York Times* critic said, "Just arrived at the gallery and having forgotten how abstract most of the Provincetown insurgents are nowadays, I mistook the conservative wall for the modern."

The two groups, and their critics, may have decided that the various forms were merging, but this is not to say that all dissent faded. One of the traditional artists removed his painting from the wall right before the 1937 exhibition opened, telling a newspaper, "It isn't an art show any more but just a place where old ladies splash their soul upon canvas and young kids exhibit their first efforts with the aid of a ten cent box of watercolors." The price of watercolors may have gone up since then, but one still often hears the comment, "My three-year-old could have painted that!" pronounced at an art opening, though not usually within earshot of the artist.

VIOLA COOK

A good whaling trip was like striking oil: a good year's catch would make you rich. Every part of a whale could be sold: the oil (the whalers pronounced it *ile*) went into lamps, and the bones became corset stays. The ambergris, scraped out of the whale's intestines, was shipped to Paris, where it was used as a base to hold fragrance in perfume. One 1910 whaling trip brought in 2,200 barrels of oil and 75 pounds of ambergris, a haul worth $47,000.

The best whaling grounds were in the South Pacific and Arctic Circle, but it took so long to reach these far-off places that a whaling trip lasted at least ten months, and could stretch on for years. Given the cost and effort of such a long trip, there was enormous pressure on captain and crew to keep going till they made their quota of whales. To "winter over" in the Arctic was a feat of bravery, or perhaps just insanity. There was almost no way out during the nine or ten months that the ice locked in the boat. Crews had to survive any way they could, insulating the boat with banks of snow, hauling sleds over the ice to find some Inuit with whom they could trade for fish and deer meat and bear hides to wrap themselves in, looking for a little warmth any way they could.

These expeditions were a calculated risk, even for the most experienced whaler. Provincetown's Captain John Cook was known not only for his successful whaling career, but also for his wife, Viola, who often traveled with him on his whaling ship, the *Bowhead*. The Cooks seemed able to survive almost anything together. One trip in the winter of 1900–1901, temperatures dropped to 57 degrees below zero, and they went fifty-eight days straight without seeing daylight. Mrs. Cook entertained herself trading tips with the Inuit women. She taught them how to sew cloth, and they taught her how to make clothes and rugs out of deerskins and bear furs. She told one journalist, "Sewing helps to dispel the monotony that will manifest itself assertively at times."

But there were times for which even a sewing kit full of thimbles and thread didn't prepare her. In June 1903, the Cooks set out again on the *Bowhead,* but the crew caught only one whale the entire summer. Captain Cook decided to winter over in the Arctic. They traded with the Inuit, but the next summer they had the same hard luck when it came to finding whales. At this point they had used up most of their supplies and food, and the crew couldn't wait to return home. But the captain, determined to fill the boat, announced that they would stay in the Arctic. The second winter, with most of the men starving and suffering from scurvy, the crew did what people do when they are being held by a lunatic—they mutinied. Somehow the captain managed to hold off the revolt. He had at least one man whipped and threw another one into the brig for the year. Viola argued vehemently with her husband about his cruel treatment of the men. Then she gave up, climbed down the ladder to her cabin, and closed the door. One account said she was "inconsolable, hugged the privacy of her cabin for weeks on end, dwelling constantly upon her isolation." She didn't come back up on deck for nine months.

In 1917 Eugene O'Neill wrote a one-act play, *Ile*, based on the Cooks' voyage. In the play, after two years at sea, the captain puts down a rebellion by the crew. His wife, Annie, begs him to turn home, but just as he finally agrees, a whale is sighted at last. The captain points the vessel north again. When he tries to explain, she ignores him and starts to play hymns on the organ while laughing hysterically. "I know you're foolin' me, Annie," the captain says. "You ain't out of your mind—(anxiously) be you? I'll git the ile now right enough—jest a little while longer, Annie—then we'll turn home'ard," he says, but he slowly realizes he has waited too long.

The *Bowhead* finally returned in April of 1906, two years and ten months after it had set out. Seamen taking part in a mutiny would normally be thrown into jail, but this was a rare case in which the captain was actually forced to pay damages to the crew for unusual cruelty at sea.

The Viola Cook who came back to Provincetown was not quite the woman who had left in 1903. Now she stood in the yard, mumbling about her husband as she brushed out his clothes and hat. Sometimes late at night, the neighbors could hear her, howling out hymns. Some blamed the experience on the *Bowhead* for her "unstable" condition, but others pointed to her husband, who had taken a mistress and showed her off freely around town. Viola spent a great deal of her time sharpening and resharpening the same unused knives, so they were like razors, just the way they should be to kill a whale. Captain Cook stayed in a separate bedroom and pushed a chest of drawers up against the door before he went to sleep, as if he were in danger of imminent mutiny inside his own house.

In 1910, Viola had recovered enough to say maybe she'd like to go whaling again, as long as it was to the tropics instead of the Arctic. Captain Cook arranged a trip south, had a new boat built, and called it the *Viola,* as if to make up for the previous voyage. The trip was less than successful: the whole crew deserted, and the limited diet onboard gave Viola beriberi, a disease caused by vitamin B deficiency, which affects the nerves, digestive system, and heart.

Captain Cook made his few remaining whaling trips without his wife; the final one aboard the *Viola* was in 1916. As for Viola, in 1922 her neighbors broke into the house after they noticed they hadn't seen any smoke coming out of the chimney for a couple of days. They found her dead on the bathroom floor; her heart had finally failed, almost twenty years after it was first broken.

THE BUILDING OF THE PILGRIM MONUMENT

There's a woman in town who sometimes spends the winter in Siena. She says she feels at home in the Italian city because every time she walks into its piazza, she looks up and sees Provincetown's Pilgrim Monument. It's no hallucination: the Pilgrim Monument, built to commemorate the Pilgrims' landing in Provincetown in 1620, was actually based on the Torre del Mangia in Siena.

Provincetowners first asked the state government for funds to build a monument to the Pilgrims in 1852. The request was turned down, and the idea went nowhere for decades. In 1892, the Cape Cod Pilgrim Memorial Association (which still operates the monument) formed as the Cape's first incorporated nonprofit organization. In 1902, after the association merged with a Pilgrim club in Brewster, the state agreed to give the group $25,000, provided its members could raise an equal amount. The matching funds came from numerous sources: a $5,000 gift from the town, the proceeds of whist parties and balls, $1 donations sent in from almost every state in the country, as well as from the Philippines. The town hall at the top of High Pole Hill had burned down and been rebuilt down on Commercial Street, so the town was free to donate the eight-acre parcel on the hill as the future site for a monument.

Members of the association spent the next three years trying to get funding from Congress before finally winning a $40,000 appropriation, which, like the state funds, came with the condition that matching funds be raised locally. There was another small string attached: the monument would fall under the control of the Department of War (now the State Department), which used it as a surveillance post in both World War I and World War II.

By 1906 the association had raised enough money to start making real plans and held a design-the-monument contest. Most of the good entries were based on the Egyptian obelisk, but the group thought too many monuments were obelisks (the Bunker Hill and Washington Monuments were two well-known examples). Instead they decided they wanted something with a bell tower, so they started researching sites in England and Holland, where the Pilgrims had spent time before coming to the New World. But they found nothing they could draw on as "traditional Pilgrim architecture," so eventually they settled on an Italian Renaissance tower. One of the best examples of this style was the Torre del Mangia, in Siena, so it became their model. Willard T. Sears drew up the plans; he was an influential architect who had worked with Isabella Stewart Gardner to design her home (now the Isabella Stewart Gardner Museum in Boston).

The association invited President Teddy Roosevelt to lay the cornerstone for the structure. On August 20, 1907, the president boarded his presidential yacht—which, by coincidence, was named the *Mayflower*—and set sail from Long Island for

Provincetown. A grandstand was erected on High Pole Hill, houses around town were decked out with bunting, and hundreds of decorated boats sailed into town. As the *Mayflower* entered the harbor, two squadrons of battleships shot off a twenty-one-gun salute, till the boats were invisible, with smoke drifting in thick clouds over the harbor.

President Roosevelt and other dignitaries rode in a big parade through town. Four-year-old Josephine Young, whose father was with the Seamen's Savings Bank, got to ride in the seat of honor, on the president's lap. The little girl couldn't get comfortable and President Roosevelt snapped at her to quit squirming and just sit in his lap. She snapped back, "You don't have a lap!" Josephine's mother, Annie, was asked what special meal she was going to make for the president. "Well, it's Friday, isn't it?" she remarked. "We always have fish cakes and beans on Friday, so that's what we're having."

Once the cornerstone was in place, construction started in earnest. Men at a Stonington, Maine, quarry loaded granite onto a boat bound for Provincetown. A crew at the wharf here unloaded the stones using a derrick and put them on a railroad car. The car ran from the wharf up to High Pole Hill, along a specially built track. At the top of the hill, workmen cut the granite, lettered and numbered each block, then followed a diagram to lay them in place. The towns of Austerfield, England, and Leiden and Delfthaven in Holland—places where the Pilgrims had stayed before they sailed for the New World—sent over special stones from their buildings. Descendants of the original *Mayflower* gave memorial stones, and the quarry in Siena sent two blocks of yellow marble to match what had been used for the Torre del Mangia. All these stones were laid on the seventeenth tier of the tower. On August 21, 1909, Isabel George, age eleven, and Annie Cromar, age fourteen, the daughter and niece of the stonework foreman, helped haul the last stone into place with ropes and a pulley.

The workmen then reversed the building process to build the inside ramps and stairs that would carry people up to the top of the monument. They had constructed a heavy wooden framework to support the staging while they worked their way up to the top, and this structure now took up all the room inside the tower. So they built the top ramps and stairs first, and dismantled the framework and staging as they worked their way back down to the ground.

One of the most amazing things about the project was that there wasn't a single workman injured or killed on the job, although there was one bizarre fatality. During an August thunderstorm, one of the railcars used to haul granite up the hill was struck by lightning. The car broke loose and picked up so much speed as it flew down the hill that it smashed through the wooden barrier at the bottom and continued across the street, hitting and killing eighty-four-year-old Rosilla Rich Bangs.

Design-the-monument contests did not end with the tower's completion. In 1977, the first edition of the excellently hip but short-lived *Provincetown* magazine published responses to a whimsical faux contest on ways to use the monument. Suggestions included converting it to a power-generating windmill to make the town electrically self-sufficient ("The blades could be 250 feet long and would make a circle 500 feet in diameter"); solving the town's parking problem ("Cranes erected at the top of the Monument could hold strands of automobiles like beaded necklaces. It would not only be functional, but pretty too"); and creating various disguises ("Cover the monument with a giant plastic replica of the Statue of Liberty. Tourist ships coming to America for the first time will think this is New York, especially when they see the prices").

One change in the Monument's appearance does take place annually. Each November, five thousand lights on three hundred-foot-long strands of wire are stretched from the top of the tower down to the ground. The switch is thrown the night before Thanksgiving, and every night thereafter until the turning of the year, the Monument resembles one of the world's biggest Christmas trees, visible for miles across Cape Cod Bay.

THE *ROSE DOROTHEA*

In a world saturated in superlatives, here is one for Provincetown: it boasts the world's biggest indoor half-scale model of a fishing schooner. Though it sounds like an arcane entry in the *Guinness Book of World Records,* this model is one of the biggest controversies facing Provincetown at the turn of this century.

Like a ship in a bottle, the boat is stuffed into the second floor of the former Provincetown Heritage Museum, the old 1860 Methodist Church at the corner of Commercial and Center Streets. Stuffed is the operative word—the schooner takes up so much space that the bow nearly hits one wall and the stern the other. You can barely squeeze around it, much less step back to get a good look at it, and the masts go up through the ceiling. At 66 feet, the model is bigger than most actual boats, but it is only a half-size replica of the 108-foot, 1905 Grand Banks schooner named the *Rose Dorothea.* The model was built primarily by Frances "Flyer" Santos, one of Provincetown's last wooden boat-builders who worked on the Grand Banks schooners, and it was completed in 1988 after eleven years of work.

All this description is moot, though, for you can no longer get inside the building even to catch an unsatisfactory glimpse of the boat. The museum has been closed since 1999, and the model of the *Rose Dorothea* is shut inside. The museum never became the tourist attraction its backers expected, the building needed extensive repairs, and its future is still in question. Town officials have considered moving the *Rose Dorothea* model out of the building. If lighthouses can be moved, they argue, why not a schooner? But some people think the only way to get the model out of the building would be with a chainsaw, and if they get it out, where will they put it? Thus far, proposals to remove the *Rose Dorothea* have been voted down.

Captain Marion Perry, who was co-owner of the original *Rose Dorothea,* would probably be turning in his grave at all the attention. He was so renowned for his prowess as a sailor and fisherman that he became a skipper at eighteen, but he was a no-nonsense kind of man, reserved to the point of being taciturn. He worked hard, but he didn't like some of the duties that went with being captain—especially having to make conversation.

He had named *Rose Dorothea* after his lovely Irish wife. When he first saw the completed boat, he almost sent it back for being too fancy. Below deck the *Rose Dorothea* was built like a yacht, with gilded moldings, polished woodwork, brass fittings, a state-of-the-art galley, and flowered curtains hanging over the portholes. "That's it," he announced. "I'm tearing it all out. It ain't fittin' in a fishing vessel." But his wife, who rather enjoyed the finery, prevailed upon him to keep the vessel as it was.

Not only was the *Rose Dorothea* way too fancy for him, but the topmast broke on its first run, which annoyed the captain tremendously.

Two years later, in 1907, a fishermen's race for Grand Banks schooners was arranged between Gloucester and Boston. Sir Thomas Lipton (of Lipton tea fame) provided the silver Lipton Cup as a trophy. People urged Captain Perry to enter the race, but he refused. "Don't I race for market most every trip? Don't I get in first? I know I got the best boat. Why should I waste time yacht racing?"

Furthermore, what would he want a big heavy cup like that for? The silver cup was worth $5,000, but so what, he sniffed, it was too heavy to drink out of.

But his wife, who was quite enamored of the race, intervened and convinced him to enter. If he won, she told him, he could just give the cup to the town.

So there was the *Rose Dorothea,* in the middle of the race, running bowsprit to bowsprit with another boat, the *Jessie Costa,* when the topmast cracked again. Captain Perry was so furious, he couldn't wait for the race to be finished so he could go after the sparmaker who had done such a terrible construction job. As it turned out, the topmast flopped down at an odd angle, dropping the sail to an advantageous position for the *Rose Dorothea.* The same sail on the *Jessie Costa* was pulling the boat to leeward, so its crew was forced to tack around. The *Rose Dorothea* just sailed straight on to Boston and won the race.

One of the crew members pulled out a broom and lashed it to the broken topmast as the *Rose Dorothea* took a victory sail for the cheering crowd. Captain Perry skipped the cheers and headed straight for his confrontation with the sparmaker.

However, after the race he was forced to suffer through further indignities. A *Boston Herald* reporter, writing about the presentation of the Lipton Cup, observed that Captain Perry was "a combination of daring and timorousnes . . . when real dangers threaten and courage and brawn and brain are needed, but . . . when men seek to haul him into the limelight of publicity . . . then he shies like a terrified horse."

The captain was so shy, the story goes, that when President Teddy Roosevelt came to Provincetown a few weeks later to lay the cornerstone for the new Pilgrim Monument, Captain Perry skipped the ceremony. Over 150 fishermen sailed in to meet the president, but Captain Perry wouldn't go. "If the president wants to see me he knows where to find me," he said.

The captain seems to have had a change of heart the next week. He heard that President Roosevelt had told the fishermen he wanted to go out fishing with them, but had to rush back to his summer home on Long Island right after the ceremonies at the monument. Captain Perry then wrote directly to President Roosevelt, saying if that was the case, he would be more than happy to take the president out for a fishing trip on the *Rose Dorothea*. It was an invitation that appears not to have been accepted.

The real *Rose Dorothea* is long gone, sunk during World War I by a German submarine. While the model is a beautiful example of wooden boat building, its craftsmanship is only one reason that people have rallied around it. During one town meeting debate over the model's fate, "Flyer" Santos, now in his eighties, said, "Don't turn your back on the men who broke their backs to win the greatest honor in Provincetown."

He was talking about something more than the glory of a sailing race. For Flyer Santos, and many in Provincetown, to lose the *Rose Dorothea* would be to turn one's back on the glory days of Portuguese sailors, and to forget Provincetown's maritime history and the long liners coming in to dock with holds full of mackerel. It would be the end of an era when people valued a quiet, hard-working fishing captain who thought more of a well-made spar than a $5,000 silver trophy.

❖

THE BOSTON POST CANE

Edwin Grozier, former publisher of the *Boston Post*, maintained, "A man who has cheated death is always an interesting figure." This was the premise behind the Boston Post Cane, the brainchild of Grozier, who grew up in Provincetown and was buried here when he eventually died in 1924.

Grozier came up with the idea of the Boston Post Cane as a publicity stunt in 1909. It became a tradition that outlasted his newspaper by decades, and one that is still carried on today, in somewhat fractured fashion, throughout New England.

Grozier first sent Boston Post Canes to the selectmen in over four hundred New England towns. A cane was to be given to the oldest person in each town. The canes were made of black ebony, shipped from the Congo in seven-foot lengths, then cut down to the right size and seasoned for six months, before being carved and polished. Each cane had a fourteen-karat gold head, inscribed, "Presented by the Boston Post to the oldest citizen of [the name of each town filled in here]—To be transmitted."

The idea was that the *Boston Post* would profile recipients of the canes, and these cameos would spur more paper sales in small towns outside Boston. The gimmick may have attracted some sales, or even advertising, but what it also attracted, often as not, was controversy. The operative phrase, it seemed, was oldest living *citizen*. Grozier equated a "citizen" with someone who was registered to vote, and, since the nineteenth amendment hadn't yet passed, this meant that only men could be recipients.

Grozier's attitude may have extended beyond legal interpretation, for he fended off demands to give women the cane even after they won the right to vote in 1920. It was only in 1930, six years after his death, that his son Richard, who took over the paper, granted women the right to receive the cane.

This opportunity was greeted by some with ambivalence. For though they had won the right to carry it, a few women wouldn't take the cane, because they would then have to reveal their actual ages. There were other reasons some people were less than thrilled by the prize: as one recipient told a reporter, "Seems to me it's not such an honor, everybody who receives it dies."

The tradition of awarding the Boston Post Cane survived even after the newspaper folded in 1957, but the custom has lapsed in a few towns. Grozier stipulated that canes belonged to the towns and were only being loaned to their recipients. He may not have anticipated the strong will—or forgetfulness—of some New England senior citizens and their survivors. The Dracut cane is still in town, but its last beneficiary (or, one assumes, that person's heirs) refused to give it back. A man in Charlton, Massachusetts, found the cane for the town of Lee in the garbage, fifty years after it had disappeared. Some towns now hold their canes captive in the town hall or historical museum.

Provincetown lost its cane for a while, but Town Clerk Sheila Silva found it in a Town Hall safe in 1993. Regular presentation of the cane has dwindled, however; for instance, after recipient Hazel Hawthorne Werner died in 2000, it took the town more than eighteen months to designate the next, albeit temporary, heir.

THE BACK SIDE

The "back side" is the name for the stretch of shoreline that runs down the entire oceanside length of the Outer Cape. The name comes from the fact that the Outer Cape's small settlements were built along the calmer waters of Cape Cod Bay, although the name seems visually apt, as well; the back side beach looks like the curve of a spine, bracing itself against the force of the waves from the open Atlantic Ocean.

While the term refers to the land that stretches from Provincetown all the way down to Orleans, you don't hear the name used much outside Provincetown and Truro. Here, going to the back side refers not only to the beach, but to the walk itself: the meandering that takes place once you cross Route 6 and head out into the dunes toward Peaked Hill or High Head. A trip to the back side conjures up, as much as anything, a sense of wild country, an outback of open moors and cranberry bogs, stands of scrubby pine and sandy footpaths a person can wander for hours without running into interpretive signs, cars, or other people. "The back country is like a wild little animal that crouches under the hand of man but is never tamed," wrote long-time resident and labor journalist Mary Heaton Vorse, a place where she could let the wild quiet "pour over me and heal me from the new, bewildering world."

SURFMAN FIRST CLASS NANCY, THE LIFE-SAVING HORSE

The coastline extending from the Peaked Hill Bars down to Monomoy is so dangerous that even with the aid of lighthouses built along the coast in the early 1800s, there were 500 officially recorded shipwrecks along that stretch between 1843 and 1859, and another 540 between 1880 and 1903. After a particularly bad winter of storms and shipwrecks along the Atlantic coast, the U.S. Life-Saving Service was established in 1872. Its crews saved the lives of approximately a thousand men off Peaked Hill in the first decades of the service's existence

Each life-saving station had its own horse, whose role during a shipwreck was to pull the surfboat and life savers down to the beach, so the men could launch rescue operations. Mary Heaton Vorse's son Heaton used to tell of the Peaked Hill Station's equine legend, an enormous gray mare named Nancy who served as the station's rescue horse from 1895 to 1910.

The station had a stable, but Nancy was too tall to fit through the door, so she had the run of the dunes as her home. She'd wander the Province Lands all day, munching on cranberries down in the bogs and nibbling blueberries off the bushes in the summer. Wherever she happened to be around sunset, she would just lie down and spend the night there.

You might think this arrangement could pose a problem for the surfmen, since they never knew if the horse would be around for a drill, much less for an actual disaster at sea, but the men of the Peaked Hill Station came up with a system to summon Nancy. Someone rang her dinner bell, and, like a Pavlovian horse, she'd come galloping across the hills at a dead run. But, as it turned out, they didn't need the bell in a real emergency. Nancy seemed to have a built-in barometer; when the pressure started to drop, she wandered over to the station. In fact, she generally spotted bad weather before the lookout did, and when he saw her coming over the dune, he knew that a storm was on the way.

Nancy performed her job masterfully, hauling the two and a half tons of crew and equipment down to the beach at a fast clip. But when she wasn't working, she was free to make her own entertainment. She was often spotted engaged in her favorite pastime: climbing up a dune, settling back on her hindquarters, and sliding down the hill, using her front hooves to steer. At the bottom, she'd roll over and stand up, shake off the sand, climb back up the hill, and do it all over again, like a kid revving up for another sledding run.

*Nancy was often spotted engaged in her favorite pastime:
climbing up a dune, settling back on her hindquarters,
and sliding down the hill, using her front hooves to steer.*

When it was time for her to be retired in 1910, the men at the station argued that, given her penchant for sand, Nancy might not enjoy her planned exodus to a government-owned bluegrass farm in Kentucky—though the more likely motive for keeping Nancy nearby was that they just liked having her around. In any event, a few strings were pulled at various levels of government, and each month, as the story goes, a check arrived at the Provincetown Post Office for one retired Surfman James Smith. The Peaked Hill surfmen took turns picking up the check, cashing it at the feed store, and maintaining Surfman Smith's steady supply of oats and bran.

Seven years after she retired, Nancy didn't show up for her dinner one day. The crew sent out a search party and found her in the dunes, covered with sand in the spot where she had fallen. There was a proper funeral, complete with stirring eulogy, out at the Peaked Hill Station, and dozens of surfmen came from around the Cape to pay their respects.

THE PROVINCETOWN PLAYERS

The Provincetown Players are now often credited for having started the modern American theater movement. But it might be more accurate to picture them, not as cultural icons, but as something out of an Andy Hardy movie: "I know, kids, let's put on a play. We could write our own scenes and make our own scenery and costumes, and use Mary Heaton Vorse's fishhouse on the wharf as a theater."

They were hardly a set of teenaged Mickey Rooneys and Judy Garlands. By 1914, John Reed had traveled with Pancho Villa in Mexico. Jig Cook had married Susan Glaspell as his third wife. Louise Bryant had left her middle-class husband and life in Oregon. Eugene O'Neill had survived tuberculosis and stints as a seaman. They had stayed up all night in bars in Greenwich Village, arguing about the validity of the war and whether the United States should enter it. Some of them were anarchists, some

Communists, most of them believed in new ideas about psycho-analysis and free love. All of them believed passionately that the theater in New York was stultifyingly constricted and dull. No one would produce the plays they were writing about the ideas that interested them.

This is how it often starts: somebody has a friend who has a friend. Mary Heaton Vorse had a house in Provincetown and urged her friends to come up from the city for the summer. The rents were cheap, the air was clear, and the beach was washed with sun. Not only that, there seemed to be a fresh wind of new ideas blowing through the world. There were the suffragette movement and the antitrust investigations, silent movies and Freud, Kandinsky and abstract expressionism. With the outbreak of World War I, artists who had gravitated to Paris suddenly had to leave. There was no going to Europe anymore, and like a series of rolling waves, the Fauvists, Cubists, Futurists, and post-Impressionists began to arrive in Provincetown.

Most of the Provincetown Players came from Greenwich Village and were friends of Mary Heaton Vorse. In Provincetown, they took turns writing and directing plays, constructing the sets, and acting; everybody did everything. They put on their first set of one-act plays in July 1915 at Hutchins Hapgood and Neith Boyce's house. The first play, *Constancy,* by Neith Boyce, was a farce based on Jack Reed's affair with Mabel Dodge. The actors used the porch as the stage, with the harbor for background scenery. Then the audience sat on the porch and looked into the house, which became the stage for *Suppressed Desires,* a Freudian satire by Susan Glaspell and Jig Cook.

After this first successful entertainment, Mary Heaton Vorse offered the old fish house at the end of Lewis Wharf as a makeshift theater. The members of the troupe dragged out the boats and nets that had been stashed inside. Everyone chipped in to buy lumber and made seats out of planks laid across sawhorses and kegs. Lanterns with tin reflectors became the stage lights. The big doors on each end of the fish house had rollers, so the door at the far end could be rolled back for the players to use the harbor as a backdrop.

The entire operation ran on enthusiasm and the spirit of collaboration. Jig Cook, who was emerging as the leader of the group, wrote, "One man cannot produce drama. True drama is born only of one feeling animating all the members of the clan—a spirit shared by all and expressed by the few for the all."

As their first production in the newly created theater, the group put on *Constancy* and *Suppressed Desires,* as well as two other one-act plays, *Change Your Style* by Jig Cook and *Contemporaries* by Wilbur Daniel Steele. That night it was raining hard as people made their way into the theater, and from time to time throughout the performance, there would be a small movement in the theater as another umbrella slipped through a knothole in the rough floor and dropped thirty feet down to the beach below.

The Provincetown Players are best known for launching the playwrighting career of Eugene O'Neill. They performed his play *Bound East for Cardiff* in the summer of 1916, using waves as sound effects. By that August, the *Boston Globe* was describing the players as "a pretty serious group" and theatrical "revolutionaries." Increasing fame for the Provincetown Players turned out to be bad news for Provincetown. At the end of the 1916 season, the group moved to New York, where the Provincetown Players got a new, more visible life in an old brownstone on MacDougal Street in Greenwich Village. Other groups have resurrected the Provincetown Players name here over the years, but the original troupe never returned to Provincetown. The Lewis Wharf, home to the makeshift theater, was destroyed by fire and storms in 1922.

EUGENE O'NEILL, GERMAN SPY?

You could see the German U-boats, patrolling the Atlantic off Cape Cod. Even before the United States entered World War I, the Germans had done their damage to Provincetown, sinking the

Rose Dorothea, the legendary winner of the 1907 Lipton Cup, off Portugal. Anti-German sentiment ran as high as fears of being torpedoed. Clearly there were potentially safer places to hang one's hat for vacation, and for a time summer cottage rentals stood vacant.

Provincetown captured its first suspected German spies on March 28, 1917, just eight days before the United States joined the war. Police arrested two men in their rooms at the New Central House (now the site of the Crown and Anchor) and charged them with vagrancy. But that was just an excuse—like arresting Al Capone for income tax evasion, or picking up "undesirables" for loitering. The two "spies" had been spotted "prowling around the radio grounds" in North Truro. One of them was carrying a black box, and it was clear the pair must be—at least could be—using this high cliff as a vantage point to tap out signals to the U-boats just offshore.

But when the police confiscated the box, they found it held, not radio equipment, but a typewriter. It turned out they had nabbed a pair of suspicious-looking artist types. One of the men was Harold DePalo, a painter. His roommate, the man with the suspect black box, was playwright Eugene O'Neill, who had dragged his typewriter out to the back shore so he could work on the beach.

After some questioning, DePalo and O'Neill were released. The *Advocate* reported that "there was nothing found or seen on the premises or in the effects of the pair to verify or bolster the underlying suspicion that the men were German spies." The incident was forgotten, though not completely. In 1918, O'Neill wrote the play *In the Zone,* which is set during the war. In the play, a British steamer is making its way through submarine-filled waters when one of the sailors onboard is accused by the other crew members of being a spy. The seaman has a black tin box, which he guards very carefully and keeps locked in a suitcase. "Did ye neverr read of the gerrman spies and the dirrty work they're doin' all the war?" asks one of the crew members. Another says, "For all's we know he might'a been signallin' with it. Ain't you read how they gets caught doin'it in London an'on the coast?"

At the climax of the play, the crew members confront the sailor, take away the suitcase, and use the key to open it. But the terrible truth locked inside the black box is neither a radio nor weapons. Inside there are only letters, which track the story of a lost romance, broken by drinking and lies. As the tied-up suspect turns his broken face against the wall, the dried white petals of a flower that has lost its scent fall out of the envelope and drift down to the floor.

❖

THE BEST DRESSED HOUSE IN TOWN

One of the most fashionable abodes in town during World War I was nowhere near Commercial Street, but a mile's walk from the east edge of town, out across the dunes toward the back shore. When the life-saving service built a new station at Peaked Hill in 1914, the old life-saving station was up for grabs to high-bidding civilians. Mabel Dodge convinced Sam Lewisohn, an investor from New York, to buy the building and have her decorate it for him. She was one of the best known of the Greenwich Village set, though her greatest accomplishments were not intellectual or artistic so much as social—she had perfected the art of the salon, drawing together a heady mix of artists and writers, Wobblies in flannel shirts and bankers in evening clothes.

In grande dame style, Mabel Dodge supervised the station's renovations from New York, while John Francis, back in Provincetown, was actually responsible for seeing that the work got done. Once the structural repairs were made, the station was redecorated in high style in shades of blue and white by Robert Edmund Jones, one of the Provincetown Players and a New York set designer. The station was a huge place by Provincetown standards of the time. It was two stories high, thirty-six by forty-two feet, with a brick fireplace, indoor plumbing, and a modern kitchen (although, like most places, it still had no electricity, only kerosene lamps).

In the end, the idea of the rugged-yet-elegant station proved more appealing than the reality for the girl used to life on Fifth Avenue. In 1919, the station was sold to Eugene O'Neill's father, who bought it as a wedding present for his son and Agnes Boulton. The O'Neills spent several seasons in the station between 1919 and 1924. It was far enough from town to be a good place to work. There O'Neill wrote much of his play *Beyond the Horizon,* which went on to win the first of his four Pulitzer Prizes. He was a great swimmer and not terribly sociable, especially when he was working. On some occasions he got away from unwanted company by swimming out as far as he could and staying out there till whoever had come by gave up waiting and went home.

O'Neill eventually moved on to other enterprises, leaving the station behind for friends to enjoy. Ray Wells told of being invited over one night for dinner by the three guys who were staying there at the time: the San Francisco socialist-novelist Hartwell Shippy; Bercovicci, a playwright; and a giant man with red hair, O'Neill's old drinking crony Terry Carlin. Being young and somewhat intimidated by the three, Wells mostly sat back admiring their alcoholic haze of a conversation about Keats. She was so shy she didn't dare interrupt, hating to break the spell of the conversation, though after about an hour and a half, she was forced to pipe up: "I had to tell them that the place was burning down," she said. One of them opened the door to the kitchen, and flames shot out. They managed to put out the fire, but "that was the end of our supper," said Wells. "We never had anything to eat that night."

It's amazing the station outlasted such nights, but it played host to a steady stream of artists, writers, editors, and various Bohemian sorts until 1931. That January, erosion finally brought the station to a precipitous position, teetering at the edge of the cliff. An early winter nor'easter did the rest, and over a period of days, the building slowly tipped over, then slid down the side of the dune till it eventually slipped into the waves. Just before it went, the critic Edmund Wilson and several friends formed a human chain, passing kitchen crockery through the top window to people standing outside, who carried it over the dunes and back to town.

JUDGE WELSH'S WRONG NUMBER

When nine-year-old John Gomes Russe came to Provincetown from Portugal near the turn of the century, he lost his legal last name, thanks to the man filling out his paperwork, who told the boy's father, "That's too many names; American people don't like all those names," and changed it to John Gomes.

The boy was so eager to become an American citizen, the moment he was eligible on his twentieth birthday, he applied for his papers, only to find that he was now legally John Gomes and could not get his last name back. He made four trips to Barnstable to argue his case, only to be told by officials, "You're wasting your time. You can only get your papers as John Gomes."

One day he ran into his former English teacher. When she asked how he was, he spilled out his frustration. "Be home between seven and seven-thirty tonight," she told him. Promptly at seven o'clock, his phone rang. "Hello, John," said the caller, "This is Judge Welsh. What the hell kind of power have you got over my wife? She orders me, the judge, to help you get your American papers." It was Judge David Welsh, one of Province-town's most prominent citizens, who had presided over cases involving such noteworthy citizens as Eugene O'Neill, but whose own humble beginnings had included a stint working as an ice cutter for an ice storage company.

Three days later John received a telegram, requesting that he come to Boston concerning his papers. He made the trip to the Mechanics Building in Boston and stood among seven or eight hundred people waiting in the hall. A voice called out his name, directing him to the booth for final papers. He explained to the woman there that it must be a mistake, because he didn't even have his first round of necessary forms yet. She looked over the paperwork. "Somebody from Provincetown," she said. "They never send anybody from Provincetown here." She then rambled on for several minutes about the various times she had visited Provincetown, asking after various people. He glanced around, a little nervous, and told her there was a big line of people waiting after him. She replied, "Let 'em wait," and kept talking.

Finally she said, "There are occasions where we make exceptions to the rules, and this is one of them. See this envelope? That's your final American papers." But there was still the matter of the test to prove his knowledge of U.S. history. "I'm going to ask you one question and one question only," she said. "I know you're a high school graduate. I hope you can answer it." She grew serious, then asked, "Who was the first president of the United States?"

Like the game-show contestant who takes his time answering a no-brainer, he hemmed and hawed, feigning ignorance. "Boy, I should know that," he muttered. She looked at him as if he were an idiot. "Wait a minute," he finally said, "George Washington?" She handed him the envelope. "Here's your papers and good luck to you."

He called Judge Welsh's house the moment he got back to Provincetown. "Judge, judge, you don't know how happy you've made me, helping me get my American papers." "John," said the judge, with just a hint of a smile in his voice, "You've got the wrong number," and hung up on the newly anointed citizen, John Gomes Russe Jr.

THE *MARGIE III*

A sagging heap of a boat showed up in Provincetown Harbor in the early 1920s. The *Margie III* had been built during World War I to chase submarines, but by the time she appeared in Provincetown, it took her half an hour just to cross the harbor. She was so listless, people placed bets on whether she'd make it back from each fishing trip. They figured it was a good thing the crew members were such lousy fishermen, because the boat would probably sink if they tried sailing in with a bigger catch. It was a wonder the crew survived at all, given how little income they eked out from fishing, though they didn't seem to be suffering from malnutrition.

All became much clearer the day a dragger spotted the *Margie III* just outside the twelve-mile limit, which marked the boundary of international waters. Instead of huffing and puffing along as usual, the boat was hurtling through the water, casting a giant wake. X-ray vision would have revealed that the beat-up, dilapidated wooden hull was just a disguise, and underneath was a steel-plated boat with four Liberty engines running, the kind that were used to power airplanes in World War I.

It seemed the *Margie III* had a secondary income, thanks to Prohibition. It never was that hard to get alcohol in Provincetown. Even when the town was officially dry, as it was during the late nineteenth century, fishermen would just stop into large ports and pick up a bottle. Back then, if things got really desperate, you showed up at the doctor's office faking a cough, and—for a fee— the doctor would write a slip that could be redeemed for a pint at Adams Pharmacy.

In most towns people remember the Prohibition era for abstinence and pretty awful home brew, but in Provincetown there was often plenty to drink. The town became a key distribution point for rum-running. Just outside the twelve-mile limit known as Rum Row, boats would rendezvous with the alcohol-laden ships going to the West Indies.

Given the *Margie III*'s engine power, she could easily outrun any patrol boats. But there was a small hitch: the *Margie III* wasn't built for hauling freight. When she was too loaded down, the crew had to stay offshore till dark, then putt-putt back into the harbor, masquerading as a tired-out old fishing boat.

As the patrol boats got smarter, so did the *Margie III*'s crew. They stayed just ahead of the law, like the Road Runner with Wile E. Coyote in hot pursuit. They lost a few shipments of liquor when they had to dump all the weight overboard to pick up speed and avoid getting caught. But after a few such instances, they improved their technique. If a patrol boat appeared, they would wrap the liquor cases in burlap, suspend them from buoys, and drop them in a line so they looked like a string of lobster pots. Then they would return sometime later to pick up the submerged cache. When the patrollers figured out this trick, the *Margie III* skipped ahead another step. They took to coating the buoys in a thick layer of rock salt to make them sink. After a few days, the salt dissolved and the buoys bobbed up to the surface, ready for a pickup.

The crew did trip up one night, when the truck coming to pick up the *Margie III*'s haul broke down up-Cape. A storm was coming in, and the crew didn't want to risk riding it out offshore. They also couldn't sail into the harbor with a hold full of liquor. So in the end they just tossed the cases overboard. The next day, every boat that could float headed out, and crews used whatever tools they could find to hook the burlap sacks that were bobbing in the bay between Truro and Provincetown. If the Coast Guard approached to board a boat, the crew would toss the load overboard, then haul it back up afterward.

The Coast Guard stopped one kayaker who was paddling offshore. What the hell was he doing in a tinker toy like that so far out? "Fishin', you gawd-damned fool Coast Guard. What the hell do you think I'm doing?"

As a show of order, the Coast Guard did manage to confiscate ten cases of bootleg whisky. The rest "disappeared," though kids could be spotted along the road the next few days, hawking Golden Wedding for 35 cents a pint.

❖

THE TRIAL OF LITTLE TIMMY

The labor journalist, war correspondent, and longtime East End resident Mary Heaton Vorse reported on most of the major trials of striking textile and steelworkers, miners, and political figures during the first half of the twentieth century. The trial she didn't cover involved a member of her own family. Little Timmy, her tan bulldog with white paws, was accused of attacking a Mr. Atwood while he was riding his bicycle. Mr. Atwood sent Vorse a summons through his lawyer, demanding that little Timmy be put down or forced to spend the rest of his life chained in the yard or locked inside the house.

This caused an uproar in the neighborhood. Little Timmy was a sort of Nanna of the East End, the caretaker of anyone who wandered into the yard to play. He led the neighborhood kids on excursions to the dunes and accompanied them across the flats on shellfishing expeditions. He also loved to go into town for the mail. In truth, the post office had started home delivery, but little Timmy missed making the trip through town, so each day he trotted off on his own down Commercial Street, to the post office and back. He had his usual stops, his rounds of barking, his appointments sniffing at the tail of this or that dog.

The charge was that Timmy had attacked the wheel of Atwood's bicycle, and knocked him to the ground. On the day of the trial, Timmy was led into the courtroom at the end of a ribbon. Mary Heaton Vorse's son, Joel O'Brien, presented the dog to the judge, holding the ribbon and lisping, "Judge, thith ith our Timmy."

Since Timmy couldn't speak in his own defense, he had to rely on his staunch supporters in the neighborhood—both adults and children. One by one, Timmy's character witnesses approached the bench and testified to the dog's kind temperament and legion of thoughtful past acts. One witness said Atwood was more likely to bite the judge than little Timmy was.

Luckily for Timmy, the two witnesses testifying for the prosecution said they had only seen Atwood fall off his bike, and that there had been a yellow dog with white legs running in the distance. This circumstantial evidence was considered too thin, so little Timmy was acquitted. However, the judge did say that Timmy couldn't travel on his own for the mail anymore.

Some time later, Timmy was exonerated entirely, when Mary Heaton Vorse's brother was out for a ride on his bicycle and "had a mongrel yellow dog run out and worry his bicycle wheels." He had spotted the real culprit.

❖

A LATE CHRISTMAS PRESENT

On December 29, 1922, the *Annie L. Spindler* wrecked on the beach near the Race Point Coast Guard station during a blizzard. The vessel had been riding low, with eight hundred cases of whisky in the hold. A hundred were tossed overboard in the storm, as the crew tried to jettison some weight, but it wasn't enough to save the boat.

Normally the Coast Guard would arrest the crew and seize the whisky as contraband since this was the Prohibition era. But because the ship was from Nova Scotia, and Canada had no Prohibition, the boat's scheduled whisky-laden run to the West Indies was perfectly legal. The captain was therefore entitled to protection under international law, so the Coast Guard, ironically, had to safeguard the whisky instead of confiscating it. They hauled the cases of liquor across the dunes by truck to a warehouse downtown, for safe storage.

Eventually another Nova Scotia ship, also with papers for the West Indies, arrived to pick up the *Spindler's* cargo. It is unclear, though, how much whisky actually made its way onto this boat. Some of the cases of liquor, it seemed, had walked away from the warehouse even while they were under guard. There was a search of houses in town, but no whisky was found. Neither could anyone show how many cases landed at their final West Indies destination. Some people claimed that the boat with the whisky merely sailed out of the harbor, then returned after dark and unloaded, returning a large portion of the original haul to the population here. Others whispered that bringing the whisky to Provincetown might have been the original plan all along, and the *Spindler's* itinerary and papers for the West Indies were just a cover in case the ship was intercepted. It's hard to say for sure; the official records of the incident were "lost."

The *Spindler's* wrecked hull kept its reputation for illicit activity. Over the years, it gained fame as an excellent make-out spot, till the remains were burned in a beach bonfire at Race Point—one lacking a legal permit, no doubt.

❖

AN AMBULANCE RIDE

Dr. Daniel Hiebert came to Provincetown in 1919 and remained the town's devoted physician until he died in 1972. In the middle of any given night he might be found in his living room attending to someone with a broken leg or a gashed head, since he made his office in his house, and the door was never locked.

Because of his dedication to his patients, Dr. Hiebert often accompanied them to the hospital if they were seriously ill. On occasion, this meant a trip up to Boston. Most people in town didn't have a car, nor could they afford the private limousine that was available, so the local hearse was frequently pressed into service to provide transportation.

Dr. Hiebert used the long trip to Boston and back to catch up on his sleep, stretched out in back next to his patient. As the doctor's wife told the story, on the way home one night, the driver stopped in Sandwich to get a cup of coffee. Dr. Hiebert roused himself from the back of the hearse at the same moment that a woman was walking by. She took one look and fainted—she thought the corpse was sitting up.

Dr. Hiebert roused himself from the back of the hearse at the same moment that a woman was walking by.

❖

SNOW DAYS

Most people will tell you the winters used to be colder in Provincetown. A heavy snow storm would separate the town from the rest of the world. People pull out pictures of the salt ice piling up on the beach, or a steam locomotive pulling into town, wearing a thick white coat of snow. They tell about the time they walked all the way across the harbor from Truro to Provincetown, aided by several flasks of whisky.

In a big snowstorm, when the town could be cut off for days, the town crier became especially important. Walter Smith once had to break the news that the Boston passenger train could make it only as far as North Truro, but not to worry, because that evening's film would be collected by someone traveling to North Truro by horse and cart, and delivered back to the Pilgrim Theater in time for the evening show.

One of the most popular entertainments after a snowstorm was sledding down Bradford Street and Medelley Hill, by St. Peter's Church. The streets were closed off to cars—though there weren't many cars at the time—and kids dressed in boots and parkas took over the road. Whole families would show up around dusk after an early dinner, dragging their double-runner sleds behind them. Some people tied together several sleds so you could fit on a dozen kids at a time, and the monster sleds, weighing half a ton, picked up terrific speed as they headed downhill. Everyone sledded into the night. If the snow started to get too thin, people would drag out a hose and spray the entire hill, daring the night to catch them on ice.

THE WRECK OF THE *S-4*

Stories about shipwrecks are part of the landscape of life in Provincetown. They conjure up images of men battered by winds, hanging from the rigging. Freezing in the ice, their fingers slip, and they fall into the freezing waves. There are houses in town capped with widow's walks, where women watched for their husbands and brothers and sons, some of whom never came back.

It is ironic, then, that the wreck whose memory remains the most poignant involved no local men. It took place, not in the dangerous surf of the open Atlantic, but right outside Provincetown Harbor. And it played itself out, not above the waves, but beneath them, out of sight.

The *S-4* was a submarine on maneuvers within sight of town, three-quarters of a mile offshore, just off Wood End. It was eight days before Christmas, December 1927. Two Coast Guardsmen, Frank Simonds and Captain Gracie, looked out from the Wood End observation tower and saw, as if in slow motion, a wreck about to happen: the submarine's periscope popped up out of the water just before a Coast Guard destroyer, the *Paulding,* slammed into it. The *S-4* sank from view, leaving only bubbles at the surface. Then a patch of oil rose and spread. It was 3:37 on Saturday afternoon, close to sunset, with near-gale force winds blowing. Captain Gracie and his crew launched a boat, raced to the spot, and dropped a grappling hook over the side, trying to hook the side of the submarine that was submerged in almost one hundred feet of water. After six hours, they found the submarine, but the grappling line snapped.

The Coast Guard sent rescue ships, the Navy sent ships and divers, and on Sunday morning they located the *S-4* again. It was too rough to send down divers, but one man persisted, dropping over the side and sinking down until he reached the hull of the *S-4*. He banged on the side of each compartment with a hammer. Only one compartment, the torpedo room, pounded back six times: six men were still alive.

The storm had abated slightly, and there was still a window of several hours to launch a rescue. There were two choices: they could drop another grappling hook and try to lift the sub to the surface, or they could hook a line and feed oxygen into one of the emergency air lines. They chose to attach a line to the rear battery room, where they thought the majority of men might be, perhaps unconscious or too weak to respond. They would pump air in and try to lift the stern to save those men.

It was the wrong choice. After an hour, bubbles started coming up to the surface, revealing the presence of a leak in the two stern compartments, which had looked undamaged but were in fact flooded, and the men in them already dead.

Diver Fred Michaels then attempted to connect the air hose to the torpedo room, where they knew there were still survivors. As he hit the *S-4*'s deck, he slid off and landed arm-deep in mud. He tugged his lifeline for help, and the officers above started pulling him up, but the line snagged on the torn metal of the wreck, pinning him in place. Then his airline caught on another jagged edge on the other side of the sub.

Another diver, Thomas Eadie, volunteered to go down to get Michaels free. Using a hacksaw, he cut away a chunk of metal to free one of the trapped lines. But just as he did so, his own suit tore on sharp metal and started filling with water. Somehow, with only minutes of air left, Eadie managed to swim to the surface, pulling Michaels up with him, a feat for which he was later awarded the Medal of Honor.

If their mission failed, at least an oscillograph was now attached to the hull of the *S-4,* so they could send and receive messages. The story slowly floated up to them. Thirty-four men were dead, and the only ones still alive were the six men in the torpedo room. They estimated they had enough oxygen to last until Monday evening.

Other rescue boats began to arrive, but it was too late. The storm had become a fierce nor'easter, and the Navy announced it was too dangerous to continue rescue attempts until the weather broke.

Relatives of the trapped men came to town, the press picked up the story, and reports of the submarine became international news. In Provincetown, lights in houses stayed on all night, and the entire town stood vigil. So many people had lost someone at sea, it was as if their own sons or fathers or brothers were pinned underwater. A private Boston wrecker offered to lend a hand, but the Navy refused: it would have broken precedent to involve a private boat in Navy operations. Meanwhile, the Navy's own wreckers sailed up from New York, hit bad weather, and lost some of their equipment at sea. Local fishermen wanted to launch their own rescue attempt, but they were rebuffed as well. The area around the *S-4* was cordoned off by Coast Guard boats to keep anyone from reaching it. The Navy rear admiral in charge even turned back the father of one of the men on the *S-4*.

People in town were furious, frustrated with the government's slow response and its refusal to mount another rescue effort in the storm. The fishermen showed their contempt by heading offshore. It might be too tough for the Navy to rescue dying men, but it wasn't so bad that they couldn't go fishing.

The truth, however, was that although it was calm enough at the surface for the small fishing boats to travel safely, any diver would have been pounded to death by the strong underwater currents. But to people in Provincetown, only one thing was clear: nothing was being done.

Messages kept coming from the crew, and those at the surface returned them, tapping out, "Your wife and mother are constantly praying for you." Early Tuesday morning, a final, weak message came back: "We understand."

Wednesday, the storm finally slowed enough to launch another effort, but by that time all the men in the torpedo room were dead. The bodies were brought out one by one and buried. It took another three months to raise the *S-4* from the bottom.

A court inquiry blamed the commanders of both the *S-4* and the Coast Guard vessel *Paulding* for the accident, as well as the rear admiral for botching the rescue attempt. The secretary of the Navy then overturned the decision, absolving both the *Paulding* and the rear admiral of any wrongdoing. The blame was shifted entirely to the dead commander of the *S-4*. To people in Provincetown, it seemed the final insult: an example of the government making deadly mistakes, then going unpunished.

Every year since then, on or near December 17, a memorial service is held at St. Mary of the Harbor Church. Taps are sounded, and the flag presented, to remember the *S-4*.

❖

SKULLY-JO

"Skully-Jo" was a Provincetown specialty otherwise known as "petrified fish." It was haddock either cured in brine or salted and dried for several months, till its consistency resembled something tougher than shoe leather, although perhaps less edible. If you didn't have a taste for Skully-Jo, you could always put it to use driving nails if you mislaid your hammer. As for durability, it lasted forever—you could chew on a piece all day and still have more or less the same exact amount as when you started.

No one is sure why Skully-Jo disappeared. The last known maker died in 1933, but, given the amount of time it took to chew a single piece, it's amazing it hasn't lasted into the twenty-first century. There was a magazine named after it in the 1970s, but the publication proved less durable than its namesake and ceased publication after a single issue. Maybe it wasn't salty enough.

❖

THE BIG BEACH CLEANUP

For most of its history, Provincetown's main dump was the beach. There weren't any separate piles designated for metal or leftover lumber or doorless refrigerators. You just threw your garbage out the window, or hauled it down to the water, and let the tide do the rest.

*That same year the practice of dumping at the beach was
permanently banned, and the massive cleanup began.*

The trouble is, the tide wasn't that thorough. Dumping got so bad that a 1941 story in the *Advocate* reported that along Provincetown Harbor, "stretches of the shore which surpassed the backyards of slum districts in slovenliness are beginning to betray the fact that there was white seashore sand under the old logs, sticks, tin cans, broken toilet bowls, discarded rubber tires, ends of rope, odd shoes, rubber boots, dead fish, bottles whole and bottles broken, rubber hose, worn out girdles, old brooms, rusted oil drums, wrecks of chairs—in fact just about anything and everything that this so-called civilization could devise to discard."

That same year the practice of dumping at the beach was permanently banned, and Irving Rogers, the town's public health officer, began a massive cleanup. But the layers of multigenerational dumping went so deep into the sand, the cleanup crew realized they couldn't clear the debris without heavy machinery. Unfortunately, the town didn't have the resources to pay for such a job, so the town auditor, perhaps in an effort to keep the budget balanced, organized a private beach cleanup fund. The Silva Trucking Company agreed to cut its normal hauling rates, and, after they removed 113 full loads of rusted-out engines, boilers, and other detritus, the beach began to resemble the stuff of charming postcard scenes again.

People still love to walk the harbor, scouring the sand for smooth-edged bits of colored glass or broken pieces of china crockery that make you wonder if someone tossed a plate through a window after an especially bad dinner. When homeowners were required to upgrade to new Title V septic systems, the front-end loaders unearthed whole bowls and cups. The pressure of the decades underground had cracked the glaze into crazy tan and gray patterns, as if they'd been fired, raku-style, underneath the sand. Once a new sewer system goes into place in town, will such treasures disappear altogether?

THE CROSS ON LONG POINT

Visitors to Long Point wonder about it, a wooden cross, taller than a man and driven into the sand, perhaps a memorial to a drowned sailor, or to one of the early inhabitants of Long Point. But it is neither; the cross has stood shivering in the wind for decades to commemorate a member of the Beachcombers' Club.

The Beachcombers began in 1916 as an all-male band of artists whose name and sensibility is reflected in a line in Robert Louis Stevenson's novel *The Wrecker:* "For the Beachcomber, when not a mere ruffian, is the poor relation of the Artist." In the early days the group mounted frequent community amusements, including costume balls, minstrel shows, and pantomimes, and the performances were noted for their off-color literary and artistic flair.

While these entertainments were often for co-ed audiences, the Beachcombers' Club has maintained its male-artist-only status since its inception, though the term "artist" is applied loosely enough to include writers, actors, musicians, and other practitioners of the arts. Members still have their own dark, beat-up clubhouse in an old fish house called the Hulk, and women are sometimes allowed in for a friendly potluck. However, the Beachcomber wife or girlfriend is left to fend for herself most every Saturday night, since the Beachcombers are dedicated to their weekly dinner with their chums, whipped up by the members, which extends into an evening of drinking, shooting pool, schmoozing, and smoking cigars.

It is this camaraderie that is most treasured by members. They built the cross on Long Point as a memorial to their fellow Beachcomber Charles Darby, who was killed in action during World War II. After Darby's death, his father wrote to the Beachcombers asking if they would honor his son's memory. "I only thought it would in some small way tie Charles more closely to his beloved Provincetown."

John Whorf, Phil Malicoat, and Roger Rilleau built a cross out of a wooden railroad tie. A bronze plaque by William Boogar was mounted on it:

Charles S. Darby
"Gallant Soldier"
Killed in Action
October 17, 1944

On a sunlit afternoon in October 1946, the Beachcombers dedicated the cross at the Art Association, across the street from the Hulk. In the 1950s, they moved the cross out to Long Point, a mile across the harbor, and stuck it in a hill of sand. Every year, some Beachcombers too young to have ever known Charles Darby take a boat to Long Point and straighten his cross.

❖

THE BLESSING OF THE FLEET

Many fishing towns around the world share the tradition of the Blessing of the Fleet, a religious ceremony to bless the local boats and ensure a year of safe and prosperous voyages.

Provincetown established its own Blessing of the Fleet in 1947, after Arthur Bragg Silva and Domingo and Edith Godinho saw a similar event in Gloucester. Provincetown's festivities went on for three days, and draggers from other towns would sail into the harbor for the blessing of the boats. The men in the fishing fleet decorated their vessels, the wharf, and a statue of St. Peter to carry in a procession. (A lot of towns honor St. Andrew, patron saint of fishermen, but Provincetown picked St. Peter, who is also a fisherman, because he's the patron saint of the local Catholic church.) The street was filled with marching bands, the Knights of Columbus and Legionnaires serving as color guards, and men carried banners bearing the names of their boats. They marched to St. Peter's for a Mass with the Bishop, then continued to the pier for the blessing of the boats. Each boat, decked in flags, passed the wharf, where the bishop said a prayer and sprinkled Holy Water over its bow. The Blessing of the Fleet was also a time to remember family members and friends whose boats had been lost in storms.

After the ceremony, families headed out to Long Point for the afternoon, boats packed with food and drinks. Over the three days there were competetive events like dory racing and tug-of-war with captains against the crews. There was a block party and dancing, with bands like Manny Silva and the Top Hatters, a fourteen-piece orchestra from Taunton, playing in Ryder Street. In later years the Linguica Band performed in their red vests, playing concertina, mandolin, guitar, and bass fiddle.

By the 1980s, people seemed less and less interested in devoting the months of planning required to organize the Blessing, and the whole event began to look more like an excuse for hard partying, as evidenced by the overflowing drinking crowds in certain bars and the influx of bikers and extra patrolmen. But in 1997, the occasion took on new life with the birth of the Provincetown Portuguese Festival. Now the Blessing has expanded into a four-day event, complete with dancing in the streets, cookouts, and a parade, with Portuguese flags and banners waving over Commercial Street. At the center of the weekend is still the Blessing itself, a Mass at St. Peter's Church, followed by the procession to the pier, with each boat passing under the hand of the bishop (or his representative) who has come to bless them all for another year. But, as with so many revivals of community traditions, the original focus of the Blessing has changed. With the fleet diminished and the fishermen's livelihoods as threatened as the species they used to fish, there are fewer and fewer commercial fishing boats to bless. Now, lining up alongside them are a wide variety of boats pitching in to keep up the tradition—sailboats and rafts, massive whalewatching boats and little molded plastic kayaks.

THE USEFUL BARKEEP

One of the perks of living in a small town is the personal service—people let you run up an account or tell you to bring the money later if you don't have enough with you. The small grocery stores around town, like the old Tillie's (which finally closed in the 1980s), would regularly deliver supplies to the local fishing boats. The cook onboard would place an order, and the storekeeper would bring the items down to the dock and load them onto the boat. This tradition went back to the nineteenth century, when the store supplied whaling boats and fishing schooners headed out to the Grand Banks.

Before the Foc'sle got sold and turned into another fern bar in 1985, it was a beat-up looking place, with tilting barstools that made you feel you'd had too much to drink even before you started. It had long been a men-only bar, dating back to its earliest incarnation as the New Deal Tavern, which opened in 1934 at the end of Prohibition. The Foc'sle was a prime hangout for fishermen, so the owners kept a ship-to-shore radio on. If someone out fishing needed to get more supplies but couldn't get back to town before the stores closed, he just called the Foc'sle on the radio. Somebody at the bar would run next door to Land's End Marine Supply, buy what the guy needed, and leave it in the bar for him to pick up when he stopped in later for a drink.

The prohibition on women in the bar lasted another quarter-century beyond the one on alcohol. The first women crossed the threshold of the Foc'sle on August 6, 1959. Owners Joe Perry and Sylvester Santos would still take orders for supplies over the phone, but, Perry told the *Advocate,* "One thing we like about the new set-up is that we no longer have to tell fibs on the phone. Now, if a fisherman's wife calls we get him to the phone instead of saying he just left or else she can come down to the place and see for herself whether he is present or not."

THE "BOYS PROBLEM"

After a 1949 *Worcester Telegram* article appeared announcing, "Provincetown 'Boys' a Problem," town officials decided to take action. The writer of the article found the postwar gay party scene quite stylish: "They are a colorful group as to attire, or lack of it, in a community which is not surprised by what anyone wears. They wear the latest sport togs, have real or synthetic suntans, and the most orderly hairdo to be found anywhere." At the same time, he reported some people were concerned, not just that gay people were starting to flock to Provincetown, but that they so insisted on flaunting their homosexuality, especially the "boys" with their drag shows.

In 1950, the chief of police decided one reason Provincetown was getting so many gay people was because business owners and landlords were so willing to employ and rent to them. So he went to the board of trade and asked for support for new bylaws so "exhibitionists" could be prosecuted. The board backed the police chief, and the selectmen came up with several new regulations, including one affecting anyone with a liquor license. It stated, "No licensee shall employ or allow to perform on the licensed premises any so-called female impersonators, nor employ, cater to, or encourage the licensed premises to become the habitual gathering place for homosexuals of either sex."

The selectmen also put pressure on residents not to rent summer cottages and guesthouses to gay people. "The selectmen have picked up the soap and gave the town a bath," stated one editorial writer who backed the new regulations. He maintained further that female impersonators were driving away "solid middle-class vacationists who didn't want themselves or their children exposed to embarrassing sidewalk scenes."

Official efforts to keep out gay people were short-lived. Some believe that Provincetown's commitment to freedom and creativity outweighed the pressures of the McCarthy era and homophobia. But as one long-time resident put it, the truth was likely more pragmatic. "Gay guys would come to town and rent a cottage in some little old lady's back yard. They were wonderful tenants. I mean, who wouldn't want them; they didn't have a lot of kids and dogs digging up the yard and screaming and drunken fights like some of the bohemians that used to move in, or the painters, who never paid their rent. This was a plum, if you could get a couple of gay guys in your cottage. They probably left it looking better than when they moved in. And you were sure of the rent. As long as you have money, dear, people are tolerant of you."

JAN MULLER'S WEDDING

In the 1940s and 1950s the Days Lumberyard was prime living quarters for many students and former students of Hans Hofmann, who'd been running his legendary art school in Provincetown every summer since 1938. Days wasn't exactly high living: there was only one outdoor toilet everybody had to share, and no hot water (or any water at all in the winter), the walls were thin, and the insulation was nonexistent. But it was a great place for painters to work, and also excellent for hanging out on the cat-walks, visiting back and forth, or piling into one of the studios for dinner and rowdy arguments over Hofmann's concepts about abstract expressionism and what he called the "search for the real" in art. "Space is not a static, inert thing," Hofmann insisted. "Space is alive; space is dynamic; space vibrates and resounds with color, light and form in the rhythm of life. Movement is the expression of life."

The space was very alive one night at Days in 1956, when Jan and Dody Muller got married. Jan was in his thirties, a fantastic painter who had suffered permanent heart damage as a result of rheumatic fever. He'd had one of the first plastic heart valves inserted, but he never really regained his health and continued to need regular medication.

The night after the wedding, Jan and Dody invited everybody over to their studio, Number 9. They put brown paper up on the walls and people drew whatever they wanted; some of the more impressive renderings were both personal and pornographic. There was a party at Days every week all summer long, and this wasn't a particularly boisterous one. But maybe it was just one too many, because somebody called the police, who showed up and hauled the men, including Muller, off to the jail in the basement of Town Hall.

Muller didn't have his heart medication with him, so he told his friend Jim Gahagan to bring his pills. The police heard the word "pills" and called in the state police, thinking there might be a drug ring at work. The men who hadn't been brought in initially now found themselves in jail. The women didn't get arrested, either because there was no matron on duty or there was just no more room in the cells. So the women led the charge to rescue Muller. They all marched down to the jail and demanded that Jan get his medication or be released. They kept this up for some time, screaming at the police. Dr. Hiebert also showed up and explained to the police why they needed to let Muller out. He added for emphasis that he wasn't going to be responsible if Jan died in the cell. When Dr. Hiebert said that if they were going to keep Muller in the cell, they were going to have to put *him* in, too, the police eventually gave in and released Muller. After everybody got out, Dr. Hiebert offered to pay for the party to continue at the Central House, but they'd all had perhaps enough "expression of life" for one night.

THE BIRTH OF THE
CAPE COD NATIONAL SEASHORE

Charlie Mayo said he knew things were changing after Route 6 was completed in 1955, because he'd see businessmen stop their cars right on the highway, get out with their briefcases, and go tromping off into the woods. Visions of postwar subdivisions were starting to dance in developers' heads, and the Outer Cape was up for grabs.

The National Park Service had begun thinking about establishing a national park on the Cape back in the late 1930s, when a park consultant investigated the possibility of a national seashore that would extend all the way from Duxbury on the South Shore to Provincetown. But Park Service budget cuts during World War II (from $32.5 million down to $5 million) stopped any land acquisition plans, and afterward the Cold War did the same.

Then in November 1956, Malcolm Hobbs broke a story in the *Cape Codder:* the Outer Cape was being considered for a new national park. It was an unusual proposition. Previous parks had consisted of land in sparsely populated areas, which was already owned by a state or public agency, or was donated, at least in part, by individual owners. This park would be carved out of an area that had been settled for centuries.

When the bill to create the Cape Cod National Seashore Park was filed in September 1959, the Province Lands became one of the fiercest points of contention. There was plenty of support for a national park, but great opposition as well, from people who believed passionately in the tradition of town-by-town home rule, from potential developers, and from town officials looking to future town growth.

The Province Lands (mostly owned by the state) covered more than 3,000 acres. The chairman of the board of selectmen, John Snow, proposed that 1,600 acres of the Province Lands be excluded from the proposed park boundaries, and the state legislature began to consider bills to cede a portion of the Province Lands to the town of Provincetown. The town manager hired a Boston firm named Van Ness Bates Associates to draw up a master plan that would look at future town needs. The firm proceeded to prepare a secret development plan for the town, but the report was leaked to the press. The plan included convincing the state to cede 1,500 acres of the Province Lands to the town, filling in wetlands north of Long Point and off Mayflower Heights, and building a golf course, high-rise apartments, a triple-decker garage, and a heliport. The plan also suggested the possibility of building a bridge between Plymouth and Provincetown.

When this proposal came out in the open, the Emergency Committee for the Province Lands quickly formed. Prominent members included Charlie Mayo, who was a selectman at the time, Josephine Del Deo (who headed the town Historical Society) prominent artist and geologist Ross Moffett, and artist and writer Miriam Hapgood Dewitt, the daughter of two of the original Provincetown Players. The group worked furiously to galvanize support for the national park and managed to win approval at town meeting for a park boundary that included all of the Province Lands.

The debate over the Province Lands still continued in Congress. In December 1960 Provincetown lawyer Ozzie Ball testified at a congressional hearing, and he seemed to sum up the beliefs of those fighting for a park that included the Province Lands: "I think the time has passed when we old-timers can hope that Cape Cod will stay the way it is," he said. "Since the park was proposed, the rape of this beloved country has begun in earnest. Therefore, we have absolute proof it is going to change, and then the issue is, should it be done by bulldozers? By money-mad people? By banks wanting to lend? By builders wanting quick jobs? By loan sharks? Or is it to be done by the U.S. government in another manner?" About the Province Lands, he testified, "If the town of Provincetown is allowed to take any portion at all of the Province Lands—and their officials brazenly propose to take its most incredibly beautiful and restful part—it will be a bloody execution removing the fountain head—indeed the very pièce de résistance."

Debate over the park continued through several sessions of Congress. The turning point may have come in the spring of 1961, when a group of congressmen traveled to the Cape to look over the land being considered for the national park. They went to Fort Hill, in Eastham, and while they stood there, looking over Nauset Marsh and discussing whether or not it should be included, someone pointed out the wooden stakes that had been pounded into the ground to mark lots for a new subdivision. On the ride back to Washington one of the senators said, "That decided it for me."

On August 7, 1961, President John F. Kennedy signed the law creating the Cape Cod National Seashore, protecting 44,000 acres of land, including all of the Province Lands.

❖

THE NIGHT THE *ADVOCATE* EDITOR GOT BUSTED

Provincetown's reputation for lawlessness gained new notoriety in 1972. U.S. drug enforcement agents made their biggest marijuana bust ever off the coast of Jamaica, just before the load was to be smuggled into the States by a group of fishermen from Truro and Provincetown.

Other drug arrests were happening all over town, and Terry Kahn, the editor of the *Advocate,* was as likely a target as anybody. For one thing, he was chairman of the board of the Drop-In Center. The Drop-In Center was an early 1970s institution where you could go for various kinds of counseling, or crash after a particularly bad trip. The center's sympathetic approach to drug use did not endear it to many in law enforcement or the town's more conservative community members. At the time, the Drop-In Center was conducting a study which would show that drug use in Provincetown was statistically as high as anyplace in the country, a fact that some in town would rather not have publicized.

The *Advocate* and its editor were also under local political fire for supporting a voter registration drive, which followed a recent Supreme Court decision that waived residency requirements. Many of the newly registered voters could therefore be just the sort of transient types who could make use of the Drop-In Center.

The editor's arrest on drug charges, however, turned out to be unrelated to any political vendetta. Truro happened to be in the middle of conducting its town census, which allows a town to purge its voting rolls of those people who have moved or died.

These days the census is sent by mail, but at that time it was done by people going door to door. Town officials didn't want to spend money to hire people for the job, so the local police had to do double duty as census takers. A fairly new recruit to the force stopped at Kahn's house and noticed a little plant growing in the kitchen. He went back to the station and returned with a search warrant.

Meanwhile, at the paper, it was deadline night. Kahn went out to get some dinner (with his lawyer, as it happened), and at some point the managing editor showed up in the restaurant, holding a clipboard with eleven names. "I don't know what to make of this," the managing editor said, "but I just got a call from the jail, and they say all these people have been arrested. I think they're looking for you."

Kahn read the names: his roommates, his roommates' girl-friends, his girlfriend. Some names he didn't recognize. It seemed the policeman had arrived during a party.

Kahn turned himself in dutifully, reporting his own arrest on an inside page of the paper's next edition. He went to court with his friends, who collectively faced fifty-five counts, including possession, cultivation, and conspiracy—an especially heavy set of charges, even for the times.

If the bust was an unlucky coincidence for Kahn, his luck at the trial proved better. It turned out that the Truro prosecutor was fighting the local selectmen over payment for his services, and he shared Kahn's lawyer, clearly presenting a conflict of interest. This left the arresting officer to argue the case, and after a bit of fumbling around in the courtroom, the judge called a conference in his chambers. The result—no convictions, seven no findings, and four aquittals—ran in another *Advocate* story, also on an inside page.

DESPERATE LIVING

Nineteen sixty-six to nineteen eighty-one. Fifteen years of in-your-face drugs and drag, whacked out movies, and periodic mayhem also happen to be the years John Waters and his friends regularly hung out in Provincetown. John Waters might hold the crown for bad-taste, low-budget movie classics, including *Pink Flamingos, Female Trouble, Multiple Maniacs, Mondo Trasho,* and *Desperate Living,* all filmed during this time period, with casts filled with Provincetown friends, among them Channing Wilroy, Mink Stole, Howard Gruber, Cookie Mueller, Sharon Niesp, Susan Lowe, Dennis Dermody, David Lochary, and a transvestite named Divine.

John used to sit in the old Dairy Queen at the corner of Bradford and West Vine working on his scripts. He still shows up there sometimes. One of his best-known gross-out movies is *Pink Flamingos,* in which Divine achieves tabloid fame as "the filthiest person in the world" and shares a pink trailer with her mother (who lives in a baby crib) and her son, who likes threesomes involving chickens. *Pink Flamingos* features, among other things, characters who sell heroin to schoolchildren, kidnap hippie girls, get them pregnant, and sell their babies to lesbian couples. "I'll tell you something," said actress Cookie Mueller in an interview. "You can rarely draw from experiences in your past for John's movies."

Another Waters movie, *Desperate Living,* had its world premiere in Provincetown. Lots of scenes from his films were shot around town or drew their inspiration from Commercial Street. There's *Multiple Maniacs,* in which Divine gets raped by a fourteen-foot lobster—one that looks suspiciously like the person in a lobster costume who used to parade around in front of the Crown and Anchor handing out flyers for the evening's show.

Off-screen life for Waters's casts was less outrageous—but not by much. One December, Divine and Cookie Mueller wanted a Christmas tree but they were broke. So they sneaked into someone's yard one night and sawed down the decorated outdoor tree. Divine was generally short on cash. He helped himself out one time by hiring a professional auctioneer, who arrived in formal attire to auction off the entire contents of Divine's summer rental, antiques and all, while his landlady was away for the weekend. For years after that, Divine had to sneak back into town to avoid the police.

Cookie Mueller always rode around town on her bicycle wearing dark eye shadow and high heels. She died of AIDS. Divine died of a heart attack, David Lochary, probably from an overdose of PCP in New York. In 1988 John Waters told an interviewer, "I hope by the end of the 90s, someone I know is still alive."

WOMAN IN THE DUNES

The oldest unsolved state police case is a murder that took place in Provincetown in the summer of 1974. The body of a woman was discovered by a thirteen-year-old girl walking her dog in the dunes about a mile east of the Race Point Beach parking lot. The dead woman was naked, her hands were missing, and her head was nearly removed.

The woman's killer has never been found, and her body has never been identified. Forensics showed the body was that of a woman between five feet six and five feet eight, twenty-five to thirty-five years old, with reddish brown hair. Because she had no hands, there could be no fingerprints. The police sent the woman's dental records all over the country, but none corresponded. They dug up her body in 1980 to take blood samples, but nothing matched.

In 1989 the police got a tip: the woman in the dunes might be a Colorado woman named Rory Gene Kesinger. Kesinger was the right height, with the right hair and the right age: she would have been twenty-five when she disappeared in 1974. She was more Bonnie Parker than a twenty-something innocent: a runaway at fifteen, a bank robber with five aliases, a user of hard drugs; she had been in jail on an assault with intent to murder charge when she escaped from the Plymouth House of Correction in 1973.

In 2000 they dug up the remains again, which were buried in St. Peter's Cemetery under a small headstone: UNIDENTIFIED FEMALE BODY FOUND RACE POINT DUNES, JULY 26,1974. Rory Kesinger's mother gave a saliva sample to investigators to see if they could match her DNA. Early tests were inconclusive but definitive. DNA tests in 2002 showed the woman was not Rory Gene Kesinger after all.

One scenario to explain the mystery goes like this: The woman in the dunes met Hadden Clark, cannibal serial killer of girls and young women. Clark, who spent part of his childhood in nearby Wellfleet, is now serving consecutive thirty-year sentences for two Maryland murders. He confessed to another prison inmate that he killed a dozen young women, starting in the 1970s, and buried some of them in the Cape Cod National Seashore. The police have brought both men to the Province Lands to see if Clark would reveal anything connecting him to this murder, but thus far, they have found no link, and they may never discover one. Clark is hardly a reliable source: the police say he thinks his fellow inmate is Jesus Christ, and he changes his stories often. Still, the theory that he killed the woman in the dunes has not yet been ruled out.

A WHALE OF AN INDUSTRY

When Al Avellar ran his charter fishing boat, he'd set up customers with bait in a spot where they were sure to bring in at least enough fish for the evening grill or the next morning's proud photos. Once in a while, a whale would surface near the boat, and then all the fishermen would drop their poles and run over to the side to watch it. This happened a lot, and, he said, "I figured if fishermen would look, there must be something to whale watching." But this was 1959, when Avellar figured, "People wouldn't pay a nickel to go look for whales."

*Once in a while, a whale would surface near the boat,
and then all the fishermen would drop their poles
and run over to the side to watch it.*

By the 1970s, though, there was Earth Day, there were SAVE THE WHALES bumper stickers, and people on the West Coast were starting up boat trips specifically to watch whales. In April 1975, Avellar took out the first whale-watching boat on the East Coast and brought along a marine biologist named Stormy Mayo to tell people something about the whales.

The trips were not an immediate hit. The whale sightings weren't great, so Avellar took to offering a case of beer to whichever fishing boat radioed over to let him know where he could find some whales.

Business slowly picked up. Avellar bought more, and bigger boats, and called them the Dolphin Fleet. His was the first whale-watching company on the East Coast but certainly not the last. These days, the New England whale-watching industry takes out about two million passengers each year, and brings in over $20 million.

Whale-watching has lost a bit of its naïve charm since the days of those first tuna boat trips. The Dolphin Fleet runs over a thousand trips a year, and a typical whale-watch has 150 people, who, armed with cameras, rush in unison from one side of the boat to the other every time another whale appears. But their frenetic desires seem invisible to the whales. They are just as majestic as ever, slapping their tails against the water over and over, as if they are exceedingly pleased with the enormous splash they can make.

A NIGHT AT THE MOVIES

The stairs were impossibly steep, the theater unbearably hot, the seats uncomfortable, and the projectionist stoned. It's the place that many people wish were still in town.

The original 1919 movie house was turned into Whaler's Wharf, a rabbit warren of little shops, portrait studios, and leather toolers. But the balcony of the old theater—110 seats up two flights of stairs—became The Movies, devoted to showing cult, classics, camp, and foreign films.

The theater looked so dingy that Frank Girolamo, who worked there as a ticket taker, said the second-most-asked question when people came up to the box office was "Is this a porno theater?" The one they asked most was "What time does the midnight movie start?"

Lots of places had revival houses in the 1960s and 1970s where you could see Antonioni, Bergman, Buñuel, and Cocteau, *Pink Flamingos* and *Harold and Maude.* But only Provincetown had The Movies.

One night it was so hot in the theater, a woman stripped down to her bra and panties. The seats were bolted down so erratically that every time a large bottom met a weak bolt, there would be a resounding crash. If the projectionist was high (which was not uncommon), the audience got a show added to the scheduled feature. The projector would seize up on a regular basis, the edges of the film would curl up and start to scorch, and the audience would scream like maniacs. One night a reel from *Fiddler on the Roof* got inserted into *Gone with the Wind,* and the burning of Atlanta segued into Tevye the milkman and his friends dancing a hora. Another time the projectionist decided to turn the projector upright, and everyone in the audience just leaned back and kept watching *Les Enfants du Paradis* on the ceiling.

The Movies' other important function was to serve as a respite from summer visitors who mobbed the streets in search of T-shirts and fudge. Most places, the hired help had to cater to the tourists. At The Movies, the official mottoes were things like "The customer is never right" and "If anything goes wrong, just leave the theater." Rudeness was endemic, as was a penchant for the staff doing pretty much whatever they wanted. One day was declared "McCabe and Mrs. Miller Day," and only hardcore Robert Altman fans were allowed in for a private screening of that grimy, snowy movie, far from the sun-bleached glare and blare of Commercial Street. The night Nixon resigned, his speech happened to fall in between shows. The staff rigged up a sound system to broadcast his speech for the audience waiting for the ten o'clock show to start, and then served free popcorn for the rest of the night.

Employees handed out coconuts to people coming to see the Marx Brothers, 3-D glasses for *The Creature from the Black Lagoon,* and bananas for a Carmen Miranda feature. There'd be some drunk person urinating on the screen, or one of the staff passed out over the counter.

An audience never knew quite what it was in for. Maybe that's what people miss most. The Movies closed in the 1980s and was reduced to serving as a storage area for shops in Whaler's Wharf, until the building burned down in 1998.

❖

Life-Saving Station on the Move

In November 1977, the National Park Service decided to save Chatham's Old Harbor Life-Saving Station by moving it up the coast to Provincetown. The station had been built on North Beach in 1897–1898, and its crew helped save ships wrecked on the Monomoy Shoals, which, along with the Peaked Hill Bars off Provincetown, was one of the worst spots in the North Atlantic for shipwrecks.

But North Beach was eroding, and the Park Service didn't want the station to suffer the same fate as the old Peaked Hill station, which slid off the cliff after a 1931 storm. To prepare for the move, they split the Old Harbor station building in two and reinforced each section with steel. On November 30, they loaded the sections onto a barge and towed the station to Provincetown Harbor. The plan was to transport the building around to the back side of the Atlantic and onto the foundation that was being built near the Race Point Beach parking lot.

There was only one problem. The day the barge left, the new foundation was inspected and failed to meet contract specifications. Everything except the footings had to be demolished, and the concrete walls needed to be completely rebuilt.

This meant that the barge would have to moor in the harbor, supposedly just for a few more days. The Park Service requested changes in the foundation plan, which led to a flurry of "I said/You never said" letters between annoyed government officials and the angry subcontractor. Unfortunately, on the second go-round he used the same concrete blocks as before without government approval, and the Park Service rejected the foundation again.

Several weeks later, a third foundation plan was accepted, and the contractor got another extension, this time until June. Meanwhile, back in Provincetown Harbor, the winter storms had done their work. An inspection of the Old Harbor station found all the damage one might expect in a wooden building that had been sitting for months on a barge in choppy seas and high winds: blown off shingles, lost sheathing, broken windows, damaged molding, interior walls starting to buckle.

A few weeks later, the newest version of the foundation was finished. The inspectors tested it out to see if it could bear the weight of the station. It couldn't, so it was rejected yet again.

The barge carrying the Old Harbor station didn't leave Provincetown Harbor until May 17. When the Park Service officials came to check out the site at Race Point Beach, they experienced what many Cape Cod homeowners arriving for the summer fear they will find: the work wasn't done. In this case, the fireplace, cistern, ramps, and porch were still unfinished, as were the concrete footings for the posts to hold the boathouse.

The project limped along, the contractor missed his June deadline, wound up working through the entire summer, and finally finished the job in mid-September.

Having taken so long to reach its new location, the station has not budged since. The Cape Cod National Seashore uses it as an interpretive site in the summer, when its rangers dress in the uniforms of the nineteenth-century life savers, and re-create their rescue drills. The station's shingles are weathered an elegant gray, and, if one didn't know its peripatetic history, one might think the building had always stood in just that spot.

THE MEAT RACK

The meat rack, the row of green benches in front of Town Hall, is the best spot in town for people watching—or for being watched. On any day warm enough to sit outside—even on days that are too cold—you'll find people lined up along the benches, short and tall, old and young, men and women, straight and gay, kids on bikes, little dogs in sweaters on laps and big dogs on leashes lunging at passers-by.

The meat rack marks the center of downtown and serves as both destination and travel guidepost, though there are subtle distinctions in its terminology. For one's own use, the spot is often referred to as "the benches," as in, "I'll meet you at the benches at seven." References to the "meat rack" are often used to describe someone else's activities, and frequently delivered in slightly derogatory or ironic fashion, as in, "Trisha and her new girlfriend are sitting on the meat rack in their Sharon Stone attire," or "Check out the guy who's holding onto his girlfriend as if somebody's going to grab her off the meat rack and deliver her into the white slave trade."

On summer evenings, the spot turns into Provincetown's version of Harvard Square, where buskers set up juggling and clown acts, drumming ensembles, saxophones and accordions. Even an eight-year-old girl, fresh from her first round of flute lessons, has been known to set down an open music case and try out a halting rendition of "Go Tell Aunt Rhody" or "Mary Had a Little Lamb" in hopes of picking up some spending money for the Penny Patch or Cabot's Candy.

Of course, not everybody likes to be so obviously on display. Those practicing cool, or who prefer observation to being observed, usually move behind the benches to the steps of Town Hall, where they can maintain a slight distance from the action. There's also more room for a game of Hacky Sack.

One person's idea of a perfect place to hang out is another's recipe for indolence and trouble, and these differing attitudes erupt every time someone tries to alter the meat rack. The police stirred up local wrath in the 1970s when they decided to remove the benches to cut down on "loitering" by what they considered unsavory types. After much uproar, the benches were returned. Even articles at town meeting to repaint or replace the benches elicit more debate than the biggest budget item on the warrant. Not too many people will argue over the relative merits of new union contracts, but everyone, it seems, has something to say about having just the right place to sit.

THE FLYING NEUTRINOS

At six o'clock each summer evening, they set up by the meat rack benches outside Town Hall, a hodgepodge Dixieland family band that called itself the Flying Neutrinos. There was balding, long-haired, snaggle-toothed Papa Neutrino, and his wife, or consort— no one was quite sure—a demure, serious-looking woman with long brown hair and glasses known as Captain Betsy. A young blond boy named Todd played trombone and tap-danced. His even younger blond sister played drums. An older girl, Ingrid, was on the cusp of adolescence, pretty with dark hair, and a slightly awkward modern dance routine that looked as if she had come up with it herself.

The family business earned the Neutrinos up to $300 a night in the summer of 1988. An audience gathered to hear them play "Sweet Georgia Brown" and "Alexander's Ragtime Band" and tossed money into the open music cases. The crowd loved them a little too much, as far as some of the nearby vendors were concerned. They complained regularly to town officials. Why should the Neutrinos get the prime buskers' spot outside Town Hall every night? Shouldn't they have to pay some kind of licensing fee the way shopkeepers did? Did all those kids really belong to that couple? Was this any way to raise a family, working on the street and living in the harbor?

Their living quarters raised as much controversy as anything. They had constructed the most amazing crazy quilt of a boat, called the *Town Hall,* from driftwood, discarded docks, pieces of condemned boats, and plenty of rope. An old generator, cast off from the actual Provincetown Town Hall, provided the power for a set of paddle wheels.

Not that the *Town Hall* traveled far; it took up residence on the beach in the West End. It was charming; it was inventive; it was carrying on the town's reputation for eccentricity. It broke the building codes; it wasn't disposing of sewage properly; it was an eyesore. The arguments continued. Eventually the board of health declared the *Town Hall* a health hazard, and the selectmen made the family move its floating home out of town. The *Town Hall* resettled just over the town line, on Beach Point in North Truro.

But the Neutrinos kept their downtown, Town Hall gig, thanks in large part to several older members of the Provincetown populace, who were among the band's most devoted fans. Even residents of the Manor nursing home on Alden Street, if they were at all ambulatory, would make their way down to Commercial Street (with the assistance of friends, canes, and walkers) to listen to the Neutrinos. Who says the elderly don't have political power? The selectmen decided to let the band play away.

Everyone said the Neutrinos were nuts when they started talking about sailing away in their floating tatterdemalion of a boat. They'd go to Newfoundland, then Europe, they said. There were abortive starts, and rescues by the Coast Guard. There were tales in 1991 that they'd made it to New York and were anchored at Pier 25 on the Hudson River. (These stories turned out to be true.) The *Town Hall* was succeeded by the *Son of Town Hall,* built in part from materials salvaged from the first boat to produce an only slightly less rickety model. And, though anyone who saw this buoyant, rattletrap scrap heap found it almost impossible to believe, the Neutrinos actually did make it across the ocean, first to Ireland and later to the mouth of the Rhône River in France.

Some of the younger Neutrinos, however, went on a different ride. Ingrid and her brother Todd grew up and formed their own band called—what else?—The Flying Neutrinos. Todd is still tap-dancing and playing the trombone, and Ingrid learned to sing. Their second recording, "The Hotel Child," was released in January 2000 and made it to number eighteen on the *Billboard* Jazz Chart.

❖

A PUBLIC SECRET

One September afternoon in the late 1980s, a woman named Sarah Woodruff appeared back in town after a vacation, driving a dark green almost-new Mercedes. She said an aunt had died and left it to her, and she had flown out to California and driven it back. She wasn't sure how she would afford the maintenance and upkeep, she said, but she kept the car and drove it slowly around town.

A few of her friends confided privately that they couldn't under-stand how she could afford it, either, though they thought it suited her somehow, with her large-boned, slightly formal demeanor and sculpted dark hair. She looked like a person of some importance, a former dignitary, who now, for unknown reasons, made her living in Provincetown selling underwriting ads for community radio at WOMR and working part-time at the Provincetown Inn.

One of her friends accidentally let Woodruff's story slip one night when he was talking with mutual friends. He thought they knew, he thought Sarah had told them, and afterward, didn't it make sense—her slightly troubled, dark air? They might have fig-ured it out from her name, Sarah Woodruff: the character in *The French Lieutenant's Woman,* who also took an alias to hide her identity.

In the case of this nonfictional Sarah, the name change was only minor, because her last name really was Woodruff. Her friends held her secret close, to keep her safe. Only slowly did they realize that it was a secret shared, it seemed, by half the town. People talked in a code of half-finished sentences that listeners had to signify they understood before the conversation would continue—phrases they would comprehend only if they knew her true identity. Once they knew what to look for, it seemed she was everywhere. A new best-selling history of the 1960s had her picture in it—she looked younger, thinner, with longer hair and no hint of the dark cloud her face now carried—but she was easy to spot.

Woodruff decided to leave town in the early 1990s, and, just before she left, she told a friend that she was thinking about giving herself up, that she had started writing about her past and might want the freedom to publish an account of her life.

In 1998, a clipping from a California newspaper showed up taped to the bathroom mirror at WOMR. It was a report that Rosemary Woodruff, ex-wife of former Harvard-professor-turned-LSD-guru Timothy Leary, had turned herself in after twenty-three years in hiding. The charges against her (helping her husband escape from jail, where he was serving time on drug charges) had been dropped. She was now working in a guesthouse in northern California. There was a brief greeting hand-written at the bottom of the clipping. It was signed *Rosemary (Sarah) Woodruff.*

SPIRITUS

After the hedges around Town Hall got cut back in the 1970s, the spot lost all value as a destination for late-night trysts. About the same time, in 1978, Spiritus Pizza moved from the middle of town and opened in the West End. It offered the perfect combination in a hangout—pizza, ice cream, and coffee for the late-night munchies, a front stoop and patio that were open to the street, and close proximity to many of the gay bars around town—the Pied Piper, the A-House, Back Street, the Boatslip, the Crown and Anchor. Maybe best of all, it had a later closing time than the bars' ridiculously early one of 11 P.M.—the hour when, if you were from San Francisco, or Chicago, or New York, or Boston, you'd normally just be heading out for the night.

The late-night scene quickly drifted west from Town Hall and took up residence at Spiritus a few minutes after last call. A 1980 photo shows people everywhere—leaning on cars, or up against buildings, sitting along the curb, standing in the street, guys in leather or with handkerchiefs strategically placed in back pockets to signify sexual preferences. In the late 1980s the police tried to break up the scene, arguing, among other things, that the crowds posed a safety hazard, because it would be impossible to get an ambulance or emergency vehicle down that stretch of Commercial Street. A few people were rounded up and arrested, there were sit-downs and menacing looks from those who weren't about to move, but it was scarcely the stuff of riots. The licensing board considered penalizing John Yingling, Spiritus's owner, for allowing such a free-for-all in his front yard. But one of the board members protested against penalizing a successful businessman for being too successful, and the whole matter was eventually dropped.

The Spiritus tradition is well into its third decade now. The bars are now allowed to stay open till one, but Spiritus's hours have also been extended to two. On any given summer night, you're likely to find several hundred people milling around the entrance, and as one summer regular reported, "I'm sure it isn't the pizza that brings them there, either." Gay guys predominate, but as many people show up to watch as to participate in what one longtime resident called the late-night "last chance for love" pickup show, complete with volunteers from the Provincetown AIDS Support Group, dispensing condoms.

Hurricane Bob

The morning of August 19, 1991, hours before Hurricane Bob hit, there was a sense of uncertainty in the air. The whole world was watching monumental developments, but not here. In the

Soviet Union a group that included Mikhail Gorbachev's own chief of staff had just launched a coup. They put Gorbachev under arrest and took a briefcase that contained the codes that would launch nuclear weapons from sites across the country.

But that international drama was muted here. The barometric pressure had dropped precipitously; the town felt underwater, the light not quite real. Last-minute preparations for the storm were being made throughout town. People rushed around, trying to tie down their boats, cross-hatching the windows of houses with masking tape to keep the wind from shattering them.

While Cape Cod National Seashore officials closed off the entrances to beach parking lots, a few hardy types took advantage of the increasing winds. Mark Birnbaum and Richard Smith went sailing past Pucci's Restaurant on their wind surfers just as the noon whistle blew.

The storm arrived about two in the afternoon, with sustained winds of 90 mph and gusts up to 120. There was an eerie, howling noise, like a wolf at the door. Flowers trembled in their vases. Boats tore loose from their moorings and crashed into bulkheads; the lucky ones floated up onto the beach. Salt spray off the high waves in the bay carried north of Bradford Street. The power and phones went out.

By 4:30 the wind began shifting around to the southwest. As it slowed down, people crept out of their houses to survey the damage. There were trees uprooted everywhere, smashed through the roofs of unlucky cars, leaning against houses, lying across roads. One of the last remaining elms in town came down, its roots yanking the earth up with it six feet closer to the sky.

There was a slightly dazed quality in the air, a combination of seriousness and frivolity, with the town struck by a hurricane but emerging relatively unscathed. Three people sat on a bench, their sunglasses cross-hatched with masking tape.

For the next week, life in Provincetown was like a trip back in time. Most of the town still didn't have any phones or electricity, which meant homes with private wells didn't have water, either. At

What's important is the costume that kills: the guy in an evening gown and train made entirely of Barbie dolls, or the team of male majorettes in sequined tutus, twirling glow-in-the-dark batons.

the end of each day, people carried more bags of spoiled food out to the garbage.

The hurricane had the strangest aftermath. Since the rain that usually accompanies a storm never came, the high winds desiccated the leaves of the trees. Overnight, it turned from summer into fall. The leaves turned from green to brown, hanging like little shrouds on their branches. Some of the plants seemed confused, and the lilacs burst into bloom, as if they thought it was spring all over again.

Three days after the hurricane, Provincetown's sole human casualty was buried. Arne Manos, one of the town's prime raconteurs, had collapsed on the street just after the storm passed. News of his death spread without the aid of phones, the story changing with each telling: he'd been touched by flying wires and electrocuted; he'd been photographing damage from the hurricane to publish in his magazine *Cape Cod Driftlines,* and a flying roof had hit him. The truth, that he had suffered a massive heart attack, proved less interesting, so the stories made their way into the local legend.

Across the world, Boris Yeltsin climbed onto a tank in front of 20,000 protesters, calling for mass resistance to the coup attempt. The crowd grew to over 100,000, including thousands of babushkas ready to take up arms. By the day of Manos's funeral, the coup had fallen, and here on the Cape, people held up signs on the street: GORBACHEV HAS BEEN RESTORED TO POWER—WHY NOT US?

CARNIVAL

Carnival arrives around the third week of August, a weeklong party that could be described as Mardi Gras in drag. The highlight is Thursday night's Carnival parade, which starts at the far East End and makes its way slowly through town. People line up hours in advance, so by the time the fire trucks and floats finally appear, Commercial Street is so jammed it's a challenge to move even a few feet for a better view.

Each year there's a different theme, like Broadway musicals or the circus or TV shows. Decorated floats appear with guys in grass skirts singing "Bali Hai" or dressed up as lion tamers, adorned with wigs and whips. But nobody really cares about the themes; each year's parade is a variation on the general theme of over-the-top outrageousness. What's important is not fidelity to the look of *Gilligan's Island,* but the costume that kills: the guy in an evening gown and train made entirely of Barbie dolls, or the team of male majorettes in sequined tutus, twirling glow-in-the-dark batons. One year a live elephant lumbered down Commercial Street at eye level with people watching from second-floor windows. Convertibles and men wearing women's bikinis are a staple.

Parade watchers in the know sport gigantic strands of green, red, or gold Mardi Gras beads. Those without the authentic necklace try to snag strands of pop beads as they're tossed from someone riding in a float. Grown-ups stand in the street screaming, "Here, here," like nine-year-olds, though mostly they're left clutching only individually wrapped gum balls or hard candy.

However much anticipation builds, a parade lasts only so long, and as the motorcycles and dogs in dresses disappear, there's an inevitable letdown. Some in the throng head off to post-parade parties, while the vast majority are left to pick up a few hard candies left in the street, or wander toward the nearest ice cream shop in search of another treat to prolong the taste of something sweet.

THE DUNE SHACKS

If you start from Snail Road, you can see them from the top of the big dune, across an expanse of sky and sand and scrubby undergrowth, out near the edge of the world. There's a flat, shed-roofed building, sitting on a rise just before the ocean. To the left of it, if you know just where to look, you can make out the stovepipe and edge of another shack, mostly hidden behind a clump of bushes.

There's no map to guide you to the shacks, but after several tries you begin to find the way, more by feel than anything else: go down to the bottom of the dune, head towards the cranberry bog, then through the pitch pines till you get to the jeep road. Most of the shacks are perched along the last set of dunes before the ocean. Some of them hug the land like a crouching animal; others rise up on stilts and shake with the slightest breeze.

The hills along the sand road are laced with beach plum bushes and *rosa rugosa,* wild beach roses with a melody of sweet-smelling, white and deep-pink petals flung wide open on dark green leaves. The compass grass waves in the wind, and the air starts to feel heavier somehow, older, as if it is holding the dense layers of experience from all the people who have stayed in the shacks over time.

Volunteers from the Humane Society constructed little huts along the back shore in the early 1800s to give temporary shelter to shipwrecked sailors. More were built by men from the U.S. Life-Saving Service, who patrolled the beaches and aided ships in trouble. The surfmen lived at the Peaked Hill Station, and the shacks provided a spot where they could bring their families, who normally stayed in town, almost an hour's walk away. A few even rigged up a fence for chickens or a cow.

The shacks were nothing fancy: there was enough room for a bed, a table, and a couple of chairs, maybe a stove and a few hooks to hang up clothes. But for anyone who liked the kind of rough, remote spareness of this landscape and the shacks, they were heaven. Many of the artists and writers who came to town around World War I found in the dunes perfect wandering grounds, where the mind could empty out completely or take off in new directions. It was a place you could go for solitude, or to bring your friends for all-night bonfires on the beach. Several artists and writers and others around town eventually bought shacks from life savers, later Coast Guardsmen. Others built their own little cottages on the shifting sand in the dunes. They passed them along to friends and colleagues, and over the decades a kind of dune culture or community sprang up.

That tradition of handing down shacks has changed forever. When the Cape Cod National Seashore was created, almost all the shack owners were technically squatters in the Province Lands, and the Seashore didn't recognize squatters' rights. After an initial battle in the early 1960s, most shack owners eventually settled with the Seashore and signed leases for twenty-five years or life. As shacks transferred to government custody, some were torn down or burned; others sat boarded up, rotting in the wind and rain.

But the fight over preserving the shacks continued for decades. In the mid-1980s, a nonprofit group called the Peaked Hill Trust formed to take care of two shacks for an elderly owner, Hazel Hawthorne Werner, and to try to convince the National Park Service that preserving and using the shacks would be better than bulldozing them. The Park Service had decided the shacks would be razed unless they had historic significance. Such a designation was to be determined by the Massachusetts Historical Commission. The Peaked Hill Trust asked that the nineteen remaining shacks be declared eligible for listing in the National Register of Historic Places. The Park Service testified against the plan, citing its 1987 analysis of the shacks, which included comments such as "Cottage's outhouse does not meet National Register listing criteria due to its recent construction, lack of architectural distinction and lack of direct associations with individuals or events significant in our past."

The Peaked Hill Trust countered, arguing that the shacks as a group served as fertile ground for the collective imagination of a kind of who's who of the twentieth century American arts scene. They drew up lists of people who had used or worked in the shacks (Edmund Wilson, Paul Taylor, e.e. cummings, Willem de Kooning, Jackson Pollock, Norman Mailer, Eugene O'Neill, Mary Oliver, Edwin Dickinson, among them) and mounted a campaign of testimonials by those who had used the shacks, ranging from speeches by local fishermen, policemen, and shopkeepers to letters Hazel Hawthorne Werner had gathered twenty-five years earlier.

Dear Mrs. Werner,

Yes, residence on the dunes at Peaked Hill Bars is uniquely sheltering and certainly stimulating to creative work. It's true that I was working on *On the Road* there, summer of 1950, and also on poems and articles.

[signed] Jack Kerouac

In 1988, the Massachusetts Historical Commission ruled that the shacks failed to meet many of its normal requirements: there were no architectural records to speak of, some of the buildings had been moved, and most were less than fifty years old. But the members voted unanimously to recommend official protection anyway. The commissioners seemed as caught up in the shacks' story as the locals were, although they were hard-put to articulate the exact reasons for their decision. "I've been struck that these buildings don't really have architectural merit," said one commission member, an architect. "But as a statement and a kind of record of a way of life, they are extremely valuable. Usually the things we deal with have a good deal of architectural significance, and this was different. This was quite unique—very unique—when a thing is unique, it's just plain unique." The keeper of the National Register later concurred, ruling that the shacks were eligible to become a historic district because of "their exceptionally significant associations with the historic development of American art, literature, and theater, and for their representation of a rare, fragile property type."

No other shacks have been torn down, but the Park Service is still trying to develop a permanent plan for them. For now, some are still in use, by individuals and nonprofit groups. And for those who come to stay, for a day, a week, or a whole season, the experience feels as it must have for their earliest tenants. "You lay in bed, you read your book, then you turn off the oil lamp," said Genevieve Martin, who has stayed in the shacks for over twenty years. "Each time you go out, you see the sky. You are in tune suddenly with the stars." "You have sand dunes and grass and a few shrubs around, and you have the wind, the water, the sun, the seagulls and the fog, and that's about it. So the kind of relationship you have with those few elements becomes very intense and very special," said Barbara Mayo.

There's still no electricity or plumbing in the shacks, just an outside hand pump for water, an outhouse, and kerosene or oil lamps for light. The sand blows under the door, through cracks in the walls. Genevieve Martin said, "Sometimes you have to turn the dishes upside down, or else you get sand in them!" The other thing you have to do, she said, is dig, or be buried by encroaching sand. In the 1970s, when Frenchie Chanel got too old to dig out her shack each year, Sal and Josephine Del Deo built a whole new shack on top of it. Now all that's left of the old shack is the green painted edge of a mural Frenchie painted, peeking out from underneath the new shack like the ruby slippers of the Wicked Witch of the East.

The sand buries everything, but the stories of those who have been there in the past still remain. There's Frenchie, who once performed with the George White's Scandals and swam out to retrieve driftwood to build a shack, tying one end of the wood to herself and the other to her black dog, Noonie, so he could swim both her and the wood back to shore. Or Dune Charlie, who lived in his shack for twenty-three years and tamed tree swallows so they'd perch in his hand. The Model A that someone drove out to visit Charlie is still in the same spot where it stalled or got stuck in the sand, rusting out a little more each year. Harry Kemp, the self-proclaimed "Poet of the Dunes," would keep a pot of stew boiling on the stove, adding more ingredients periodically. One time he got down toward the bottom of the pot and pulled out the glove he used to light the kerosene lamps. "Thank God!" he said, "I never knew where I lost it."

"I feel the presence of other people having been here, and I wonder about them," said Marilyn Pedalino, after she had slept out in one of the shacks. That feeling continues sometimes even after you leave. One woman was walking home, back up the big dune, and saw a coin in the sand. She picked it up and noticed it was worn soft at the edges, with a woman's face on the front. It seemed foreign at first, but then she saw the date, 1935, and real-

ized it was a Liberty dime. It had probably been dropped sometime back then, and, like the dune shacks, had been waiting out
there ever since for the next generation to come and find it.

SOURCES

Albee, Peggy A. *Old Harbor Life-Saving Station, Provincetown,
Massachusetts: Historic Structure Report.* U.S. Department of the
Interior, National Park Service, North Atlantic Region, Cultural
Resources Center, Building Conservation Branch, 1988.

Baker, Susan. *The History of Provincetown.* Burlington, VT: Verve
Editions, 1999.

Barnstable County. *Three Centuries of the Cape Cod County:
Barnstable, Massachusetts 1685–1985.* Barnstable, MA:
Barnstable County, 1985.

Berger, Josef. *Cape Cod Pilot,* Provincetown, MA: Modern Pilgrim
Press, 1937.

Bradford, William. *Of Plymouth Plantation, 1620–1647.* New York:
Capricorn Books, 1962.

Brooks, Ben. *Days Lumberyard Studios* (Exhibition Catalogue).
Provincetown, MA: Provincetown Art Association and Museum/
Shank Painter Printing Company, 1978.

Burling, Francis P. *The Birth of the Cape Cod National Seashore.*
Plymouth, MA: The Leyden Press, 1978.

Buzzard, Robert Guy. *The Geography of Cape Cod.* Doctoral disser-
tation, Clark University Press, Worcester, MA, 1965.

Cook, Lurana Higgins, Hugh Francis Cook, Anne Gleason
MacIntyre, and John Stuart MacIntyre. *Provincetown
Massachusetts Cemetery Inscriptions.* Bowie, MD: Heritage Books,
1980.

Corbett, Scott. *Cape Cod's Way: An Informal History of Cape Cod.*
New York: Thomas Y. Crowell Company, 1955.

Dalton, J. W. *The Life Savers of Cape Cod.* 1902. Reprint, Orleans,
MA: Parnassus Imprints, 1991.

Del Deo, Josephine. *Figures in a Landscape: The Life and Times of the American Painter, Ross Moffatt 1888–1971.* Virginia Beach, VA: The Donning Company Publishers, 1994.

Egan, Leona Rust. *Provincetown as a Stage: Provincetown, The Provincetown Players, and the Discovery of Eugene O'Neill.* Orleans, MA: Parnassus Imprints, 1994.

Finch, Robert, ed. *A Place Apart: A Cape Cod Reader.* New York: W. W. Norton, 1993.

Gaspar, Frank. *Leaving Pico.* Hanover, NH: University Press of New England, 1999.

Green, Eugene, and William Sachse. *Names of the Land: Cape Cod, Nantucket, Martha's Vineyard, and the Elizabeth Islands.* Chester, CT: Globe Pequot Press, 1983.

Hatch, Isabel. *The Log of Provincetown and Truro on Cape Cod, by Mellon C. M. Hatch.* Provincetown, MA, 1939.

Huntington, Cynthia. *The Salt House: A Summer on the Dunes of Cape Cod.* Hanover, NH: University Press of New England, 1999.

Jacobs, Michael. *The Good and Simple Life: Artist Colonies in Europe and America.* Oxford, England: Phaidon Press, 1985.

Jennings, Herman A. *Provincetown, or, Odds and Ends from the Tip End.* 1890. Reprint (facsimile edition), Provincetown, MA: Peaked Hill Press, 1975.

Johnson, Joyce. Interview with Ray Martan Wells for oral history program "Sands of Time," WOMR Radio, Provincetown.

Kittredge, Henry C. *Cape Cod: Its People and Their History.* Boston, MA: Houghton Mifflin, 1930.

———. *Mooncussers of Cape Cod.* Boston, MA: Houghton Mifflin, 1937.

Lawson, Evelyn. *Yesterday's Cape Cod.* Miami, FL: E. A. Seemann Publishing Company, 1975.

Mitcham, Howard. *The Provincetown Seafood Cookbook.* Reading, MA: Addison-Wesley, 1975.

Moffett, Ross. *Art in Narrow Streets: The First Thirty-Three Years of the Provincetown Art Association 1914–1947.* 1964. Reprint, Provincetown, MA: Cape Cod Pilgrim Memorial Association, 1989.

Mourt's Relation: A Journal of the Pilgrims of Plymouth. Originally published in 1622 as *A Relation or Journal of the English Plantation settled at Plymouth.* Edited by Jordan D. Fiore. Plymouth, MA: Plymouth Rock Foundation, 1985.

O'Neill, Eugene. *Eugene O'Neill: Complete Plays 1913–1920.* Edited by Travis Bogard. New York: Library of America, 1988.

———. *Eugene O'Neill: Complete Plays 1920–1931.* Edited by Travis Bogard. New York: Library of America, 1988.

Provincetown Historical Association. *Here's Provincetown/ Provincetown Historical Association.* Provincetown, MA: Provincetown Historical Association, 1979.

Quinn, William P. *The Salt Works of Historic Cape Cod: A Record of the Nineteenth Century Economic Boom in Barnstable County.* Orleans, MA: Parnassus Imprints, 1993.

———. *Shipwrecks around Cape Cod: A Collection of Photographs and Data Covering the Period from the late 1800's to 1973 on Cape Cod.* Farmington, ME: Knowlton & McLeary, 1973.

Reffe, Candice, ed. *From the Peaked Hills.* Provincetown, MA: Peaked Hill Trust, 1988.

Rich, Shebnah. *Truro—Cape Cod, or, Land Marks and Sea Marks.* Boston, MA: D. Lothrop and Co., 1883.

Seckler, Dorothy Gees, edited with a foreword by Ronald A. Kuchta. *Provincetown Painters 1890's–1970's.* Syracuse, N.Y.: Visual Arts Publications, 1977.

Seligson, Susan V. "How They Found the *Portland.*" *Yankee,* December 1989, pp. 68–75, 120–25.

Shay, Edith and Frank, ed. *Sand in Their Shoes: A Cape Cod Reader.* Boston, MA: Houghton Mifflin, 1951.

Smith, Nancy W. Paine. *The Provincetown Book.* Brockton, MA: Tolman Print, Inc., 1922.

Snow, Edward Rowe. *A Pilgrim Returns to Cape Cod.* Boston, MA: Yankee Publishing Company, 1946.

Thoreau, Henry David. *Cape Cod.* Boston: Ticknor, 1864.

Trayser, Donald G. "Once upon a Time on Cape Cod." *Cape Codder,* October 7, 1948, p. 2.

Vorse, Mary Heaton. *Time and the Town: A Provincetown Chronicle.* New York: The Dial Press, 1942. Reprint, Provincetown, MA: Cape Cod Pilgrim Memorial Association, 1990.

Ward, Nathalie/Center for Coastal Studies. *Stellwagen Bank: A Guide to the Whales, Sea Birds, and Marine Life of the Stellwagen Bank National Marine Sanctuary.* Camden, ME: Down East Books, 1995.

Willison, George F. *Saints and Strangers: Being the Lives of the Pilgrim Fathers & Their Families, with Their Friends and Foes.* Orleans, MA: Parnassus Imprints, 1945.

Wilson, Edmund. *The Twenties.* Edited by Leon Edel. New York: Farrar, Straus & Giroux, 1975.

———. *The Thirties.* Edited by Leon Edel. New York: Farrar, Straus & Giroux, 1980.

Frequently consulted: *Cape Cod Times, Provincetown Advocate, Provincetown Arts, Provincetown Banner, Provincetown* magazine (Louis Postel, publisher, 1977) and Pilgrim Monument and Provincetown Museum archives, www.capecodaccess.com. Of particular help were the *Provincetown Arts* articles "What Time Does the Midnight Movie Start?" by Dennis Dermody (1997–98 issue); "High Art, Low Art and Trash: Notes and Nights from 'The Movies'" by Frank Girolamo (1993); "The Cross at Long Point" by Amy Whorf (1991); and the *Provincetown* magazine articles "Former Advocate Editor Talks about Being Busted" by E. J. Kahn III, and "Eugene O'Neill: Playwright or German Spy?" by Mick Rudd (vol. 1, no. 1, 1977).